BUILD A DISCIPLINED ORGANIZATION CULTURE

Using

MissionWon™

WAYNE HERNANDEZ

authorHOUSE®

AuthorHouse™
1663 Liberty Drive
Bloomington, IN 47403
www.authorhouse.com
Phone: 1-800-839-8640

First published by AuthorHouse 11/21/2011

ISBN: 978-1-4670-8147-4 (sc)
ISBN: 978-1-4670-8148-1 (hc)
ISBN: 978-1-4670-8149-8 (e)

Library of Congress Control Number: 2011919124

Printed in the United States of America

ENDORSEMENT:

Any organization wanting to grow its business and excel needs to build a solid foundation. One of the pillars supporting it is the people. It is the cornerstone of the architecture. Your institution's success begins with them. Your organization's success is measured by the success of your employees. The chapters in this book <u>Build a Disciplined Organization Culture Using MissionWon</u>™ by Wayne Hernandez provide the vision and the valued discipline for building the blocks of success. It is a laddered approach.

It is a tried and proven approach as illustrated in the chapters of this book. The book outlines the techniques and provides understanding in depth for climbing the ladder of success to both management and employees through a planned methodology. Each Strategic Goal is a platform. In the laddered approach, when one Strategic Goal is achieved each subsequent Goal raises the bar to the next level of success to achieve both for management and employees.

<u>Build a Disciplined Organization Culture Using MissionWon</u>™ illustrates the right tools for every organization. MissionWon™ is a "must" for anyone to reach the pinnacle of success and achieve Financial Success through growth and productivity.

Dr. Mario Thuraisamy, PH.D.

TO MY FAMILY AND WORK ASSOCIATES

To my wife Claudia, children, Nicki and Lauri, parents, Herbert and Lynette, and my entire family for their patience, support and guidance; my work associates who contributed to the development of this process in particular Chock Petchprom and all former MCI (bought out by WorldCom) employees who worked on the Sugarland Local Service team and proved beyond any doubt that MissionWon™ works. It worked so well that out of twenty-two departments; five of the top ten yearly accomplishments for the Vice-President of the Dallas Super Center came from the Sugarland team. My boss, David Amador, the managers, supervisors, and employees who took MissionWon™ and not only made a name throughout MCI for themselves but made a tremendous impact on their customers, stockholders, and themselves. I would also like to thank the authors that I read for any ideas or thoughts I may have used that helped put MissionWon™ together.

A special recognition goes to my father, Herbert Hernandez, for all of his leadership, discipline, and encouragement he instilled in my personal and athletic life. Based on his guidance I learned how to put discipline as a top priority in my life and sports' accomplishments. I also need to give my mother, Lynette Hernandez, recognition for her guidance in my life and for her work in editing the manuscript for this book.

"<u>A Culture of Discipline</u>:
WHEN YOU COMBINE A CULTURE OF
DISCIPLINE WITH AN ETHIC OF
ENTREPRENEURSHIP, YOU GET THE
MAGICAL ALCHEMY OF GREAT
RESULTS"

JIM COLLINS

"DISCIPLINE IS THE BRIDGE BETWEEN GOALS AND ACCOMPLISHMENTS"

JIM ROHM

PREFACE

Most managers today don't plan, don't share their plan, or do not involve their staff with input into their plan if they do have one. If any of this hits home, you need to seriously take advantage of the process, MissionWon™ that I developed while working on my Masters Degree from the University of Southwestern University, now known as the University of Louisiana, Lafayette.

After my tenure as Director of Telecommunications of the State of Louisiana, I realized all of the mistakes that we made and decided that these would never happen again. Unfortunately I was not given much leeway to be a very good manager. I was told what to do and how to do it from above even when they did not know the details of our problems or what the potential solutions to solve them were. We also wasted many hours in meetings with 20 or more staff. As you well know, this does not work very often, and it did not work most of the time for us. We had no direction because my entire staff had never seen or had any input into the strategic plan that was put into my boss's desk drawer and mine. The only time it was used was when he wanted to act on an issue. We lacked DISCIPLINE.

I then developed the MissionWon™ process because I knew that everyone in the organization needed to have some input into our day-to-day actions, along with a document that they could look at to see where we were headed and how we were going to get there. I wanted my staff to have DISCIPLINE. If I could accomplish this, I knew that each of my employees would understand where we were headed and many of them who wanted to participate in the process would take ownership of the process and make it successful. I developed MissionWon™ as part of my Masters Program and gave my presentation for about 3 hours. After my presentation, I was asked but one question and that was by the head of the Chemistry Department. His question was, "Wayne, this looks great, I believe it will work for all businesses, not just telecommunications. Will this work for business in general?" My answer was a definite, "Yes, it will work for all businesses."

I proved this was true in numerous management positions I held later, but none had as big an impact as we had with my two years in Houston, TX as a Sr. Manager with MCI. My initial boss was located in Dallas, and he told me that I could manage the organization the way I felt that I needed to. That gave me the opening to use MissionWon™. You will see what we did in the book to make improvements that we needed to make to strengthen every one of our measurements every quarter for two straight years. He told me that before I took over, he would get complaints daily about that section and its numerous problems. After about four months of my taking over, he did not get any complaints at all. What were we doing that had such a major impact? He even took about ten of my staff to Dallas to help them do a better job implementing what our team was doing in Houston. Even with the loss of these key people, we still got our measured numbers down from the previous quarter every quarter.

The Vice-President e-mailed each of his 22 Sr. Managers to inform him five of their accomplishments for the previous year. I sent him five of the many accomplishments we had done for the previous year. At his annual meeting with his staff he announced his organizations top 10 accomplishments. I am proud to say that all five of my staff's accomplishments were in his top 10 accomplishments for the year. Not bad when you understand that about 150 people out of about 3,000 had half of the accomplishments of their Vice-President. These people took the MissionWon™ process, implemented it, and their actions really stood out. Even the President of the company, who had over 100,000 staff, made reference to these 130-150 people in her yearly speech when she said, "If you have the best numbers for provisioning, you should share your process with others." Our team showed their DISCIPLINE and stood out amongst 40,000 employees.

Once you have finished this book please go to http://www.missionwon.net for additional information.

Table of Contents

1

Why Build a Disciplined Culture?

" 'Giving Orders' instead of 'Requesting and Establishing Commitment'-
Ownership and excellence do not come from order takers, and usually
ordering produces resentful avoidance, when what we really want is the
ownership, pride, and passion that comes when people commit to what they
are doing"

Robert Dunham's Top 14 Mistakes Senior Managers Make

MissionWon™ meets the above statement because it does not give orders but
requests and establishes comment from employees who take ownership,
pride, and passion because they commit to what they are doing.

Before we get into the details of creating a disciplined culture, we
must first convince ourselves that a disciplined culture is better than a non-
disciplined one. As a quarterback on my high school football team, I can
remember my father, who was the head coach, constantly telling us that we
had to have discipline. We had to have discipline as individuals first and that
would translate into a disciplined team. Everyone on the team including the
water boys knew exactly what they had to do, when they had to do it, and
precisely how to do what they were assigned. If any one of us failed in our
assignment we not only let ourselves down, but also our team. Needless to
say, we were determined to accomplish our goals as we went undefeated that
year.

I can still see the picture of the two donkeys tied to a single rope trying to eat
hay from two separate piles just out of reach. In the next frame they pulled at
each other but the rope held them back from the different piles of hay that
they attempted to get to. Finally they put their heads together to come up

with a solution that worked for both. In the fifth frame they both go together to one pile and finish eating it. In the sixth frame they go to the other pile to eat it. Teamwork and discipline were learned from that poster.

In one football game my end, Rusty, came into the huddle after the first play of the game. He told me that the defensive back was slow and that he could beat him. On the next play I told him to go deep. He did and made a touchdown. This is one example of why listening to input pays off. The next time we were on offense I told him to go deep again. He scored again. We did the same thing the next two times we got on offense. I threw the ball four times, all to Rusty, who scored four touchdowns in the first half. Both of us were sent to the bench in the first half because the coach did not want to run up the score. At half time Rusty and I were told that we could go in for one series, then we would have to go back to the bench. I told him to go deep. Yes, he made the fifth touchdown with my fifth pass. We were then sent back to the bench, which did not bother us. Our backups needed to get to experience play in the games. They practiced and needed a chance to play also. Our goal was to make a touchdown every time we had the football. It shows that we had discipline and a team goal. It did not matter who made the points, but that we meet our goal as a team. This shows that Robert Dunham is correct when he says " 'Giving Orders' instead of 'Requesting and Establishing Commitment'-Ownership and excellence do not come from order takers, and usually ordering produces resentful avoidance, when what we really want is the ownership, pride, and passion that comes when people commit to what they are doing."

That must have had a big impact on us because we won the State Championship for the first time in the school's history. We may have been one of the smallest teams; but we were the most disciplined, both as individuals and as a team. That discipline paid off because not only do we have great memories of our accomplishments, the discipline that we learned from those experiences remains with us throughout our careers and personal lives.

Jim Collins' book, GOOD TO GREAT, studies the differences between companies which over the long run became GREAT companies and similar companies that failed to meet the standards set by these Great companies. Of these, some remain today as mediocre while others are either out of business or have been bought out. Throughout his research, words such as *disciplined,* rigorous, determined, consistent, focused, accountable, and responsible kept coming up in discussions with members of organizations that later were determined to be in those "Great" Organizations. These descriptions were not raised in discussions with people in those organizations that did not break out and become one of those "Great" Organizations. As per Mr. Collin's conclusion, "Indeed, discipline by itself will not produce great results. We find plenty of organizations in history that had tremendous discipline and marched right into disaster, with precision and in nicely formed lines. No, the point is to first get self-disciplined people who engage in very rigorous thinking, who then take disciplined action within the framework of a consistent system designed around the Hedgehog Concept."

Mr. Collins also states: "*A Culture of Discipline*. All companies have a culture, some companies have discipline, but few companies have a *culture of discipline*. When you have disciplined people you don't need hierarchy. When you have disciplined thought, you don't need bureaucracy. When you have disciplined action, you don't need excessive controls. When you combine a culture of discipline with an ethic of entrepreneurship, you get the magical alchemy of great performance."

By disciplined, we don't mean in the tyrannical sense, but in the terms of freedom and responsibility within a given framework as described in <u>GOOD TO GREAT</u>. To make the case we can look to a number of long-term successful businesses, organizations, sports teams, business leaders, coaches, and leaders of numerous countries. They can attest to the fact that over the long term, the vast majority of successful leaders build and maintain *disciplined organization cultures.*

Think about today's leaders who have built successful countries and companies versus those who have built long-term failures. Tyrannical discipline is successful only in the short term. When the dictator is no longer in power, the organization both crumbles and goes away, or a completely new leader comes in who struggles to remain on top and usually fails in the long term. Look at countries such as the former Soviet Union and its history versus the United States. Take corporate examples with high profile CEO's who are the center and focus of every decision that happens in their organization. Think about what happened to Chrysler when they lost their "high profile" CEO. I am not saying that he was a tyrannical boss, but Chrysler was not a disciplined organization because everything revolved around him -- he was "Chrysler." When he started to back out of running the day-to-day business, the business started to go down. Chrysler had no method in place to have a smooth transition from one administration to the next. Because MissionWon™ builds a disciplined organization, the transition from one leader to another is seamless no matter his or her background. The only time this will not occur is if the new leader totally abandons MissionWon™. A smooth transition can be accomplished if the new manager makes his own modifications to the existing planning methodology. This type of transition results in minimal impact on employees, customers and investors.

In his book, Mr. Collins describes a number of benefits of having a disciplined culture: with disciplined people we don't need hierarchy, with disciplined thoughts, we don't need a bureaucracy, with disciplined actions, we don't need excessive controls, and a disciplined culture creates a flywheel effect within the organization that continually builds momentum. The advantages are that our management teams and their staffs can spend more time being proactive and less time being reactive. Any bureaucracy can be minimized; thus allowing employees to spend more time being productive and with fewer controls. Our employees are less restricted in their actions and thus more productive with their accomplishments.

Once this planning methodology is implemented and the culture becomes disciplined, most of the day-to-day problems are eliminated as they are addressed and accomplished on a proactive basis. When you finish reading this book, you will understand how a disciplined culture will eliminate the majority of problems and daily decisions that result in managers in your organization having more time to address new problems.

So, just how do we achieve this framework of disciplined people, having disciplined thoughts, and taking disciplined actions? We build a culture around the idea of freedom and responsibility within the framework of this planning methodology called MissionWon™.

2

Why A Planning Methodology?

"The reason most people never reach their goals is that they don't define them, learn about them, or even seriously consider them as believable or achievable. Winners can tell you where they are going, what they plan to do along the way, and who will be sharing the adventure with them."

Denis Waitley

MisssionWon™ meets this statement because each member of the team can define, learn, and believe his ideas are achievable. Your team will certainly be a winner because they can tell you where they are going, what they plan to do along the way, and who will be involved in sharing the adventure with them.

The team that uses this knows where they are going, what they are doing along the way, and all of their employees will share in the adventure and success. You may be asking yourself, "Why should we use a planning methodology, named MissionWon™, to build a disciplined culture and just why and how was it developed?" We will begin by answering the question, "Why use MissionWon™ to build a disciplined culture?" The answer will also become obvious in Chapter 11 when you see the results that are achieved when the methodology is implemented.

I could give you the short and obvious answer by telling you that you should use it because it delivers results. This will become obvious when I show you the results from two companies in which I implemented MissionWon™.

In a paper, "The Detrimental Effects of Power on Confidence, Advice Taking and Accuracy," by Kelly See and Elizabeth Morrison, NYU Stern Professors of Management, and colleagues studied survey data from hundreds of working professionals across a range of organizations and industries. One of their conclusions was that individuals with greater power discounted even valuable advice. The reason was because these individuals had an elevated confidence in their own initial judgments. Additional conclusion was that "the very power entrusted to these individuals may introduce a mindset that prevents them from taking advice, and thus from making sound decisions." MissionWon™ has a major impact because it promotes input and recommendations from everyone in the organization. It then allows the upper levels of management approval or disapproval of the input and recommendations of their organization. They are able to utilize their power through the approval process while receiving input and recommendations. Bottom line; they can make sound decisions that insure that their Mission is accomplished.

We can start with some of the advantages of this planning methodology. To begin with, it insures that no time or money is being wasted on projects or changing processes that don't contribute to the overall Mission. When we finish the process of identifying all of the Projects and Changes in the way we are doing business today, we can see how each of them contributes to accomplishing the Mission. Once this process is complete, we should not be making any changes or working on any projects that aren't identified in this planning methodology document. Since your document will be continually modified and updated as required. Any of these Changes should be approved and documented in your plan. Secondly, MissionWon™ improves communication with your employees in view of the fact that the plan is documented in simple terms and posted for everyone to see. Next, employees know at all times the direction of the company. It also improves communication and employee morale when managers provide feedback on a monthly, quarterly, and yearly basis, to their sharing with them _their_ accomplishments. At this same time managers go over Goals that need to be accomplished in the next month, quarter, and/or year. Employees have the ability and mechanism to take ownership by having input into the process and the opportunity to identify and solve their own problems. They are also able to see where and how their efforts contribute to the company's direction and success. The MissionWon™ methodology also improves the use of resources, as managers are easily able to track and allocate resources to accomplish higher priority projects that are pre-approved and prioritized. The need for meetings becomes minimized as all Goals and Projects are identified and approved in advance. New projects that do not fit in the MissionWon™ plan either are dropped prior to major discussions, or if deemed to fit into the plan, are identified and approved by upper management through an approval process and added to the plan or dropped as appropriate. Your management team can spend much more time on being proactive versus being reactive. Fewer controls need to be put in place. Everyone in the organization understands his role and is focused on the Goals and Projects that have been identified.

One of the major benefits of the MissionWon™ planning methodology is that it creates a mechanism to achieve a flywheel effect of continually building momentum and creating recurring results as mentioned in <u>Good to Great</u>. Visualize a large flywheel and the amount of energy it takes to get that heavy flywheel moving. The movement is very slow at first, but gradually starts to move little by little. As the flywheel speeds up, less and less effort is required to make it go faster. The faster the flywheel goes, less and less energy is required to improve its speed. The same holds true for MissionWon™. Most of the energy is put into developing and implementing the plan, which starts out slowly. As the project begins moving along, less and less time and energy is required. The faster and larger impacts that come from the methodology are being felt both internally and externally to the organization. Implementation of MissionWon™ also stimulates change and progress by making employees think about their problems and identifying and taking appropriate action or actions to solve them. It also focuses the entire organization on accomplishing your Mission and builds a "Team Atmosphere" between managers and employees. It improves communication through employee participation. It documents Goals so that everyone within the organization is aware of what the company's Goals (and theirs) are and how the Projects they are working on contribute to the company's Mission. They understand why they are spending time doing what they're doing and why it is important. MissionWon™ empowers employees by giving them a venue for positive input, responsibility and ownership in solving their problems. And most importantly it insures positive impacts on all areas: customers, employees, and stockholders.

Now let's answer the question of why and how it was developed. It started when I was Director of Telecommunications for the State of Louisiana. As Director, I had overall responsibility for the planning, designing, procurement, installation, maintenance, and continued upgrade of all of the State's telecommunication facilities. Included in these responsibilities were a fifty million dollar budget and over one hundred and eighty employees. I do not mention these to brag, but to give you a feel for the number of problems that I faced every day. Can you imagine? OK, and then double it because at that time in history, the breakup of the Bell System had just occurred and everyone was flying by the seat of his or her pants. There were no books written on the subject as there were in the data processing field. We had all sorts of inexperienced vendors getting into the telecommunications industry. Not a pretty sight! To top it off, we were what are called self-funding agencies since we got no funding from the State Legislature. In other words, we had to operate just like a telephone company; we had to generate our own funds by charging the various state agencies for our services, collect the funds, pay our vendors, and pay our internal operational expenses including salaries. In addition we still had to provide improved service and at a lower cost than each agency could procure on its own initiative. If we couldn't do that, the agencies would have gone to the Legislature and had us disbanded. Translation: 180 civil servants, including yours truly, would be looking for jobs (not my idea of a fun time). To top that off, I also had a boss who had one person reporting to him--me! Yes, he had a boss who had two people reporting to him along with me (that relationship was only on paper, I really reported to the top boss). As you can imagine, each of them had WAY too much time on his hands! Did I mention that both of my bosses' backgrounds were in data processing? Analog and Digital had not married yet. Big problem? You bet! Faced with all of these you can imagine the number of problems that plagued my staff and me. These caused so many meetings that my secretary would page me to tell me that I needed to leave the one I was in to attend another one that had already started. This was also causing a tremendous strain on my staff, as most of them were in numerous meetings every day also. We had hundreds of projects going on but were wasting most of our time in non-productive meetings. Very little was ever accomplished in these meetings and very little was being accomplished on our projects. Not providing the agencies with timely telecommunications services was causing more and more problems due to the backlog that continued to grow.

Before I took over as Director, my boss and his boss had engaged a consultant to develop a strategic plan to cover the State's telecommunications needs. For a cost of about my yearly salary, we got a document that was about 50 pages of pretty generic gobbledygook, most of what was already being done. After my two bosses and I read the document and concluded it contained nothing that we could use, it was put in the bottom drawers of our desks and never saw the light of day again. Even if we had used it, no one else would have ever seen it. So the staff had no direction. No matter, none of our employees had any input into the process; so any solutions that were contained in the document might solve upper management's problems. But the odds were that they would have minimal impact on our employees' day-to-day problems. Even if we had given everyone a copy, due to its complexity, ambiguity, and sheer volume, none of the employees would have had the time to read and understand this entire document. So we as mangers took the parts of the plan that we liked and kept it in our heads. No, we didn't all like the same things so we had three separate plans. Had our employees known what was in our heads, maybe we would not have had to have one meeting after the other. How many employees do you know who like to spend their Fridays until 6 P.M. or later in meetings? Let me tell you from first hand experience, none that I know of. I am included in that none. Guess how much we accomplished in those meetings! Zip! Nada! Only when the head knocker dictated that we all agree on what he wanted to do would we come to a single decision.

So, now you know the background that led me to wondering if there were ways to solve all of these problems. I knew that I wasn't the only manager who had these types of problems but had no clue of how to solve them. I knew that whatever the solution was, it had to be fairly simple, easy to implement, have input from the employees and the results were available to them. It also had to be a working document and not static. That is when I started talking with a friend of mine from Graduate School, Chock Petchprom. He suggested that I use a format similar to one he was using in the data processing field. After reviewing his recommendation, his basic format met my requirements of being simple, structured and easy to understand. We then discussed ways we could interface a planning structure into this format and came up with the basic structure, which has since become the basis for what is now called MissionWon™.

As part of my Masters Degree in Telecommunications, my project explained what is typically included in classic telecommunications Strategic Plans, Tactical Plans, and Operational Plans. How difficult it was to see how, if ever, the cohesion is between all three. (If a Tactical Plan has no relationship and/or commonality to the Strategic and Operational Plans, then it will be extremely difficult to manage a disciplined organization since everyone is singing from a different songbook). I also introduced my newly developed planning methodology and explained the advantages it had over the traditional method. When I finished my three-hour presentation, only one member of my committee, the head of the Chemistry Department, had a question. He said that it looked as if my planning methodology could be used for any type of strategic, tactical, and operations planning, not just for telecommunications planning. My answer was simple, "Yes, it will work best in a business planning scenario." Since then, I have used it as a business-planning tool and as a planning methodology within a department in a major business. In both cases the results were outstanding and could not have been achieved in such a short timeframe without using this methodology.

3

Start With Value Discipline

"Success demands singleness of purpose."

Vince Lombardi

MissionWon™ addresses the above statement because every one of the employees or members focuses on a single purpose – To achieve their Mission.

We must now determine what central value we are going to provide to our customers. Once we determine this value, it will shape the decisions that follow throughout our planning methodology and thus throughout our organization. In their book, <u>The Discipline of Market Leaders: Choose Your Customers, Narrow Your Focus, Dominate Your Market</u>, Michael Treacy and Fred Wiersema identify and discuss the new rules of competition and the three value propositions. They state that these rules dictate that we must be disciplined and focus on one of three standards that have been established in today's marketplace. If we are to be leaders in our field, we must put unequaled value in the marketplace. This can be accomplished by insuring that we focus our disciplined organization on that one value that we chose, but at the same time still meeting threshold standards in the other dimensions of value. Once this value is established, we must continue to reset these standards year after year. And finally, we should build a superior operating model in order to deliver this value. This decision should be made prior to setting up your Mission so that it can be incorporated into your Mission Statement.

Now that we have established the basis of how we intend to focus on value in building our plan, let's discuss the different forms of value that we should choose from as identified by Mr. Treacy and Mr. Wiersema in their book. Today's market leaders choose from one of the following three central values from which they focus all of their plans and strategies around:

1) Operational Excellence
2) Customer Intimacy
3) Product Leader

Operationally Excellent companies offer their customers dependable products or services at competitive prices, delivered with minimal difficulty or inconvenience. They provide value to their customers with a combination of quality, price, and ease of purchase that no one else in their market can match. They do not cultivate one-on-one relationships with their customers nor do they develop lots of new products or services (if any at all). Their management systems focus on integration, reliability, high-speed transactions and compliances to norms. Their culture is built around rewarding efficiency. At the same time they despise waste. Think about Wal-Mart, McDonald's and Dell Computer and how they develop the value that they put in the marketplace.

To become a **Customer Intimate** company you must focus on cultivating your relationships with your customers. You must make it your business to know your customers and the products and services that they need. You should continually tailor and upgrade your products and services to meet your customer's needs. You consider your customer's lifetime value, not just the profit and loss on a few transactions. You should also focus on making money by tapping the unrealized potential in your client's operation. Your main obsession is with the core processes of solution development, results management, and relationship management. You must build your company's business structure around delegating decision making to your employees who are closest to the customer. Management systems are geared toward creating results for carefully selected and nurtured clients. Focus on embracing specific rather than general solutions and thrive on lasting relationships. You should be very client driven, proactive, change-oriented, and proud of your superior knowledge of the application of your products. Customer Intimate companies measure their successes by the level of their customer's success. If your customer fails, then you fail also. If your customer succeeds then you succeed. You want to be seen as a member of your customer's organization. You should be crafting complex solutions and integrating them into your customer's businesses with sophisticated account teams and specialized service and product support groups. In order to provide this value to your customers, you must maintain a very broad product line that is easy to configure to meet specific customer needs. You should embrace solid, tested products that can be tailored to fit your customer's needs like a glove. You should produce unmatched value to your clients who don't necessarily want the very latest, just the best result and help in obtaining and implementing it. In summary, to be a customer intimate company you should:

1) Form yourself to fit your customer's needs
2) Your management systems should be based on complete measurement of your account's penetration–set Goals for penetration, expansion, and growth
3) Spotlight not on profitability or market share, but on your share of your customer's expenditures–which requires exact, meticulous, and integrated customer data
4) Your key target is your "Share of their Customer"
5) Your principal disappointment should be to "Lose a Client"
6) Don't market products on the bleeding edge
7) Depend on a stream of products that are characterized by evolutionary enhancement, not evolutionary transformations
8) Provide stable, controlled, incremental improvement of your products coupled with the proficiency that leads your clients through changes in their application and management

Should you determine that your company or department should focus on being customer intimate, Managing The Professional Service Firm, will provide insight and numerous goals that could be used. Many of the Goals we used for the networking firm came from this book. Examples of companies that focus on customer intimacy are Cable & Wireless and Airborne Express.

Companies that fall into the **Product Leader** category consistently strive to provide their market with leading-edge products or useful new applications of existing products or services. They continually challenge and focus themselves in three ways:

1) Creativity is prevalent
2) Their ideas are rapidly commercialized
3) They persistently pursue ways to improve their own latest product or service

To become a Product Leader, focus your operating model on the core processes of invention, product development, and market exploitation. Make your business structure loosely knit, ad hoc, and continually changing to adjust to the entrepreneurial initiatives and redirections that characterize working in unexplored territory. Management systems should be results-driven and measure and reward product success. The value put forward to your customers is that your company presents the best products, period. Examples of these types of companies are Cisco Systems, Intel, and Federal Express. In summary, product leaders:

1) Continually strive to provide leading-edge products or new applications in using existing products or services.
2) They persistently challenge themselves.
3) Their core focus is on invention, product development, and market exploitation.
4) Their business structure is loosely knit and varying to adjust to entrepreneurial initiatives.
5) Their management systems are results-driven and they measure and reward themselves by successful new product creation.
6) They offer the best products on the market and look at themselves as their biggest competitor; therefore, they attempt to constantly put out better and better products.

Now that we have an understanding of what the different types of market leaders are and how each operates, let's look at the similarities that make them market leaders. First, each one of them provides the best offering in the marketplace by excelling in a specific dimension of value. Second, each maintains a minimum threshold standard on the other dimensions of value. In other words, they don't allow their performance in other dimensions to slip so much that it impairs the attractiveness of their company's unmatched value. Remember the Yugo lowest price–but poor quality and service. That is a good example of not keeping up that minimum standard in the other value dimensions. Third, they dominate their market by improving value year after year. They don't just deliver today's best products; they deliver tomorrows and the next day's best products. And finally, their operating model is committed to deliver unmatched value. This is the key to raising and resetting their customer's expectations. By continually improving their value, they make their competitor's offerings look less and less appealing and may even destroy their market position by rendering their competitor's value obsolete.

The Discipline of Market Leaders: Choose Your Customers, Narrow Your Focus, Dominate Your Market covers the above in much more detail. It should be read by those members who will chose the company's or department's value discipline that will be used to focus the Mission Statement and Goals of the planning methodology.

Once we have determined our value discipline, we should incorporate it into our Mission Statement. This way we assure that we focus the majority of our actions on insuring that our employees understand our chosen value discipline. By doing this they focus on this value as they develop the plan.

4

The Mission Statement

"If you don't know where you are going, any road will get you there."

Lewis Carroll

MissionWon™ meets the above statement because all employees have input into direction the company, division, or department is going with their Mission and how to achieve it efficiently and successfully.

The basic configuration of MissionWon™ starts with our Mission Statement. By starting with the Mission Statement we insure that all Goals in our Strategic, Tactical, and Operational Plans are structured towards accomplishing the Mission. As discussed earlier, in conventional planning processes the Strategic, Tactical, and Operational Plans are usually all separate documents and most of the time they have little or no synergies between them. It is difficult to comprehend how the Operational Plan feeds the Tactical Plan and how the Tactical Plan in turn feeds the Strategic Plan. Even more difficult to understand is how the Strategic Plan insures that our Mission is accomplished. If we carry out our Operational Plan, does that translate into achieving our Tactical Plan or are there additional actions required to fulfill the Tactical Plan? The same principle holds true for our Strategic Plan. What about our Mission Statement? Is our Mission being fulfilled as we complete our plans? Think about it. If we aren't accomplishing our Mission by completing our plans, then either that Mission Statement we have posted is not a good one or our plans aren't up to the standards that they need to be to insure that our organization is on a proactive track to success. Since the process starts with and is based on our Mission Statement, it is of utmost importance to formulate precisely what needs to be addressed in our Mission Statement. If we are using this process to build a corporate plan or just using the process to build one for a division, a department, or other entity, such as an athletic team or organization: the Mission Statement should be developed with the following fundamentals in mind.

There are a number of philosophies on what should be in Mission Statements and even how long or short they should be. In order for MissionWon™ to fulfill our needs we must insure that our Mission addresses three things, not necessarily in any particular order. First, we must address our customers. Without customers, either external or internal, we will not remain in business very long. No matter if we are using MissionWon™ for an entire company, a division, or a small department, we can still identify who our customers are. If we are using this methodology for a sports team our customers may be our fans or the members of the team. Think about it. In most cases (not all) without the fans we probably would not have a team. We should identify how we are going to provide our products to our customers in our Mission Statement. We will go into further discussions in Chapter 6 on the focusing of our Mission Statement on certain principles and the major structuring of our Goals to insure that we adhere to these principles.

Secondly, we must address our employees. In more cases than not, our employee is our most important asset; therefore, we must make sure that these assets are treated as such. Our employees have a major impact on the value that we present to our customers, either through their part in putting the product or service together, or by their direct interaction with the customer. In either case we need to have disciplined employees putting their best foot forward at all times. Production defects or below standard customer service will not establish a good reputation in the market for our company. I have spoken to many business consumers of services who are very dissatisfied with their vendor's services and have either replaced them or are in the process of looking for alternatives. Think about how much it costs to get a new customer versus keeping an existing one. Marketing costs and sales commissions are high budget items that are minimized on existing customers. Think about the timeline required to sell and bring a new customer on versus an existing customer placing an order. Remember our employees have a direct impact on our customers and our customers have a direct impact on whether or not we remain in business. Therefore both of these must be part of our plan; and since it starts with our Mission Statement we must include them in it.

The third entry in our Mission Statement is our investors. Bottom line is if our plans don't include Goals that make our company profitable then we will not be in business very long. There are not many investors who can afford to lose money for very long and even fewer who will continue to invest in a company that does not provide a return on their investment. They will find other places to put their money where they will receive a higher return. As capital is pulled from the company, more negative happens than positive. It is a downward spiral that is hard to reverse. One CEO (Chief Executive Officer) who told me that he insured that his company met their Mission by continually meeting with the employees and working on details. His company's stock, which is traded on one of the major stock exchanges, had gone from the $50 range to the $4 range in the previous two years. My understanding is that the company is no longer in business. I doubt that any of his stockholders would agree with him that they were accomplishing their Mission. Bottom line is: we must address our investors in our Goals and Mission Statement.

Now that we have identified the three major elements that we must address in our Mission Statement, let's look at a couple that were actually implemented. (I've underlined the three things that need to be addressed.)

> **MISSION - "To Deliver Outstanding <u>Customer Service</u> Through Customer Intimate Value Disciplines, to Provide Fulfilling Careers and Professional Satisfaction to Our <u>Employees</u>, and to Achieve <u>Financial Success</u> Through Growth and Productivity"**

This Mission Statement was developed for a networking company that sold wide area network hardware and engineering services. As you can see from our Mission Statement, we addressed our customers by stating that we wanted "To Deliver Outstanding Customer Service Through Customer Intimate Value Disciplines." We addressed our employees with "to Provide Fulfilling Careers and Professional Satisfaction to Our Employees." And finally, we addressed our stockholders with "to Achieve Financial Success Through Growth and Productivity." We added a broad scope in each to focus on how to accomplish each part of the Mission. This gave us guidance as we started to chart out our Goals.

Here is another example of a Mission Statement that addressed the three major elements.

> **MISSION - "To Deliver World Class Customer Service through Operationally Excellent Delivery Systems, to Provide Fulfilling Careers and Professional Satisfaction to Our Employees, and to Improve Shareholder Value."**

Once again notice that we address our customers, our employees, and our shareholders. This Mission Statement was developed for one of five CLEC (Competitive Local Exchange Carrier) departments of one of the largest telecommunication companies in the United States. This department was located in Sugarland, Texas. This particular department had Order Entry and Project Management, along with Translations and Provisioning Engineering responsibilities to provide local telephone service to medium sized companies throughout the United States. The other four CLEC departments for this company were located in Fredrick, MD; San Antonio, TX; Dallas, TX; and Tulsa, OK.

The following is the Mission Statement of the School Board MIS Department where I was the Director. Notice in it that we addressed the taxpayers, our users, and our employees.

> **MISSION - "To Insure the School Board's Information is Recorded and Maintained on a Timely and Cost Effective Basis Using Appropriate Resources and Accessible to the Appropriate Personnel While Providing Fulfilling Careers and Professional Satisfaction to Our Employees"**

David H. Maister discusses Mission Statements in his book, Managing the Professional Service Firm that we used as a template for developing the three

34

above Mission Statements. We also used many of the ideas in his book to develop the Goals that were used in our plan for the networking company since we wanted to focus on services. I would definitely recommend this book for all managers in the services field.

We can now look back on our examples of Mission Statements from earlier. In the first one we had, "To Deliver Outstanding Customer Service Through Customer Intimate Value Disciplines...." By putting through customer intimate value disciplines in our Mission Statement, we set a clear direction that we intend to focus on customer intimate values as we develop our Goals through our planning. Since this Mission Statement was developed for a "Services Led" company where they sold expensive networking hardware and highly experienced and technical engineers' services, it makes sense to focus on customer intimacy principles. Notice in the second Mission Statement example, "To Deliver World Class Customer Service through Operationally Excellent Delivery Systems...." we state that we will focus on operationally excellent values throughout our Goals. This Mission Statement was developed for an organization whose main function was to take a service order and manage it as a Project from the time the order hit our desk until the engineers turned the service up to the customer. It was different from the customer intimate company in that our main focus was to get our customer up and in service as soon as possible. Another difference was that we did not deal with the end user directly, but through field service teams throughout the United States. Had these service teams utilized MissionWon™, they may have focused on being customer intimate. This may or not be the case for all service organizations, but most would fall into this category.

Now that we have developed our starting point with our Mission Statement, we can begin to develop the rest of the building blocks of MissionWon™. Although a consultant can be used to act as a facilitator in the discussions to insure that all phases are followed and documented, anyone who has read this book and has good management experience and can facilitate the discussions can lead this Project. The time required is higher at the beginning of the Project and tapers off to mostly a maintenance mode once it becomes operational. From past experience, I recommend that the uppermost level of management take ownership of rolling out and promoting MissionWon™. The overall results will be proportional to the level of ownership promotion by upper management and buy-in by the employees of the organization. The bottom line is the higher in the organization the process is rolled out and promoted, the larger and sooner the results start to pour in. We will address more about the results later. Our main point here is that the highest-ranking manager in the organization implementing MissionWon™ should be the main promoter. This is not to say that it has to be rolled out to the entire company.

It works just as well within a division or department when it is rolled out and promoted at those levels also. We implemented it within the Sugarland, Texas, CLEC Department with only 130-150 employees; and our results earned the attention of the President of the company. In her yearly speech to her 40,000 employees, she mentioned that each department should share its best practices with other departments. Although she did not mention us by name, she went on to say that if a department had the best provisioning numbers in the company, they should share their processes with other provisioning departments. We knew she was talking about us because our provisioning numbers were 17 days when we started just like everyone else, but in the past year and a half we had gotten them down to less than five days. None of the other CLEC departments had provisioning numbers below 17 days and none of the long distance provisioning teams had improvements of this significance. Shortly thereafter, her Senior Vice-President sent one of his staff to find out what we were doing to make our numbers so much better than everyone else's. They were looking for one or two things, but through our use of MissionWon™, we were doing a lot of little things that amounted to major accomplishments in all areas of our business. He never got the answer he was looking for. They were looking for short cuts, but there were none. We explained to them that we had implemented this planning methodology that resulted in major improvement in of our areas of operation. But upper management failed to recognize how we accomplished our successes. They wanted a simple solution. There was a simple solution: MissionWon™. It identified our Goals, the problems we faced in accomplishing them, and finally the solutions and actions needed to achieve those Goals. Unfortunately, no one above our department recognized that implementing MissionWon™ across the board would have empowered their employees to make major improvements to all phases of their organizations.

When our Vice-President, who had 22 departments, sent an e-mail to each of his 22 Sr. Managers asking them to give him their top five accomplishments for the past year. I sent him Sugarland's top five. When he announced his Center's Top 10 Yearly Accomplishments at the awards banquet, five of them came from the 130-150 Sugarland CLEC employees. These 130-150 employees out of approximately 3,000 produced 50% of the Super Center's largest yearly accomplishments. Imagine what could have been accomplished had the other 22 departments used this planning methodology. Think about what could have been accomplished had the other 115,000 company employees used MissionWon™! Don't believe bankruptcy, once WorldCom bought us, and major layoffs of the company would have been the end result!

5

MissionWon™-A Planning Methodology

"Almost always, the plan is too complex. Too much to learn in too little time."

Vince Lombardi

MissionWon™ meets the above statement because it is simple and easy to understand.

Traditional planning consists of different types of plans including Strategic, Tactical, Project Plans, Operational Plans and Disaster Recovery Plans. In MissionWon™ we are going to take the first three and combine them into one comprehensive plan. This simplifies our plan and insures that all of them come together as one.

In the traditional planning process, we have no method of insuring that once we complete our plans we will complete our Mission. How do we connect our projects to our tactical plan? Does the Tactical Plan include all of our projects? Or are we working on projects throughout our organization and hope they are positively impacting it? Are all of our managers checking into whether or not every one of the projects that his staff is working on is called for in our Tactical Plan? Maybe the first question should be is, "Do we have a Tactical Plan?" Then we can ask, "Are our managers aware of it and following it?" If we are committing resources to projects that aren't called for in our plans, then we are not utilizing our resources to their fullest potential. We are not going to have the most impact on our Mission by wasting resources on projects that have minimal or no impact on it. The same can be said about the relationship between the Tactical Plan and the Strategic Plan. Are we sure that our Tactical Plan directly relates to our Strategic Plan and if we work our Tactical Plan, then our Strategic Plan will be accomplished and also our Mission?

These are some of the questions and problems we want to eliminate in MissionWon™. We need to make sure that every project that our staff works on will have an impact on our Mission. If not, then we should ask ourselves why we are working on it? If it doesn't impact our Mission then we are not utilizing our time and/or resources to their fullest potential. When we waste resources, we are not accomplishing one of the major components of our Mission -- our stockholders. How many of our stockholders don't care if we waste resources? My guess is none.

MissionWon™ will consist of Strategic Goals that will address each of the three parts of our Mission Statement. These Strategic Goals will be long range and high level. Figure 1 shows how our Strategic Goals are related to our Mission.

Figure 1

Once we identify and approve our Strategic Goals, we will identify Tactical Goals for each of the Strategic Goals that we have previously identified. These Tactical Goals will be shorter in time frame and more detailed than the Strategic Goals that they address. Figure 2 shows how our Tactical Goals relate to our Strategic Goals.

Figure 2

Once our Tactical Goals have been identified and approved, we will then identify and approve Projects or Changes in the way we do business that will make each of our Tactical Goals happen. Figure 3 shows how our Projects or Changes in the way we do business relate to our Tactical Goals. Although they are listed as Projects, they may be Changes in the existing processes or the way we are doing business in today's environment.

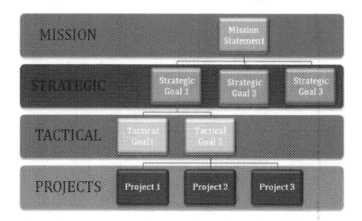

Figure 3

If we were using MissionWon™ for a large organization with a number of different departments, our model would look like Figure 4. We will identify each different division and department's responsibilities by specific color differentiations.

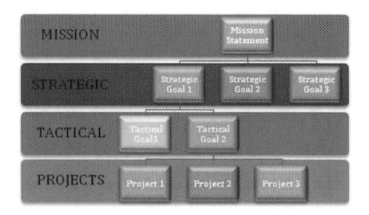

Figure 4

Now that we have developed our Mission Statement and determined which value discipline to focus on, we are ready to move into the next phase of the process. We are now going to assemble the Strategic Goals portion of MissionWon™.

6

Strategic Goals

"Build for your team a feeling of oneness, of dependence upon one another, and strength will be derived from the unity."

Vince Lombardi

MissionWon™ meets the above statement because it is developed and implemented as a TEAM approach providing that oneness feeling with dependence upon one another, and strength from unity.

Prior to the working sessions, all employees in the organization should go to a MissionWon™ presentation. This presentation or presentations for larger organizations should be presented, or at least attended, by the highest-ranking manager. This is important, as it will communicate to all employees what the overall process is and their roles in its success. The process is very simple but the results are significant. The more knowledge and understanding the employees have of the process, the better the participation. The better the participation, the better and sooner the results are achieved.

Just as in typical Strategic Plans, the time frame is long range, usually three to seven years in length. These Goals should be high level and broad in scope. Strategic Goals should be well thought out and address at least one of the three things in our Mission Statement. Strategic Goals should be developed in working sessions of the two highest levels of managers from the company, division, or department that the plan is being developed for. A facilitator should moderate these sessions to insure structure and adherence to the process. There can be as many Strategic Goals as necessary to insure that the Mission Statement is accomplished. There must be at least one Strategic Goal for each of the three things addressed in the Mission Statement. In reality, you should have a number of Strategic Goals for each.

In discussions on all Goals, managers should always take into consideration the value disciplines that were previously decided upon. This means that the majority of the Goals will be designed around that value discipline although there will still be Goals developed around some of the other value disciplines. Remember we still have to meet minimal standards in the two other values. Just as important, we need to discuss the high level problems that we are experiencing or anticipate experiencing in the future. In discussing these problems, we will also discuss possible high-level solutions. The solutions that are ultimately agreed upon will be translated into our Strategic Goals. Remember at this level we are working at the highest levels and the details will be worked out in later sessions. This is an extremely important phase because we are working on setting the direction for all of our future sessions.

Let's look at what information we need to identify in our sessions for each of these Strategic Goals.

- GOAL: A general description of the Goal.
- PRIORITY: Rank the Goal on the basis of importance in relation to other Strategic Goals. More than one Goal may be assigned the same priority.
- SCOPE: The scope must be in enough detail so that anyone in the organization reading it will understand its intent.
- TARGET DATE: Since these Goals are long range, they should be at least three years out. This date can be either estimated start dates or completion dates, but they must remain consistent. It is difficult to set a specific target date for these since they are long range. Remember this is a working document and this date can be changed, so make your best estimate. Many of these will be continuous throughout the lifecycle of the plan; so many times the response to this will be "on going." You may also want to identify a quarter such as "third quarter of 20XX."
- PROJECT LEAD (S): This should be the project leader or person or persons responsible to insure that this Goal is accomplished. Since this is a high level Goal, it should be assigned to a high level manager with the authority to insure that the Tactical Goals and in particular the Projects are accomplished. It may be that the majority of the project's managers are members of his/her organization. This would insure that he not only has the responsibility, but also the authority to make sure that progress is being made on this Goal. You may even want to assign this to a group of managers, i.e. All Sr. Vice-Presidents.

- <u>CURRENT STATUS</u>: This should be a roll up summary from the current status of all of the Tactical Goals that feed this Strategic Goal.
- <u>COST</u> (if any): This is a best guess of the total costs of the Projects that feed this Goal. This will be done after all of the Tactical Goals and Projects are identified and costs estimated.
- <u>IMPACT STATEMENT</u>: This statement will identify any impact either positive or negative or both that this Goal will have on our Mission. Example - - If this Goal is not accomplished by July, we estimate that we will be unable to provide services to our European markets. Example - - If we accomplish this Goal by July of 20XX we will overcome the governmental restrictions that will allow us to continue and expand our European markets. Example - - If customer retention continues to decline, our stock price will decrease.
- <u>% TO COMPLETION</u>: This is the average of the % To Completion of the Tactical Goals that feed this Strategic Goal. Although this is never perfectly accurate, it will give upper management a good estimate of where they stand in respect to accomplishing their Strategic Goal.
- <u>Approved By</u>: This would be the name of the Manager(s) who approved the Goal along with the date of initial approval or the date of approval of modifications.

Let's look at our Mission Statements and some of the Strategic Goals that were generated to guide our accomplishments. Some of the completed Strategic, Tactical Goals, and Projects are not listed.

MISSION - "To Deliver World Class Customer Service through Operationally Excellent Delivery Systems, to Provide Fulfilling Careers and Professional Satisfaction to Our Employees, and to Improve Shareholder Value."

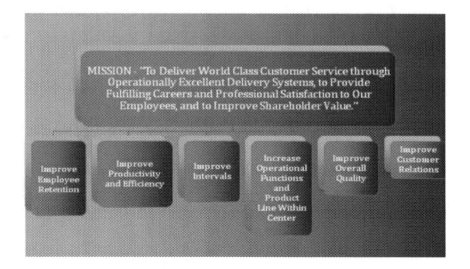

STRATEGIC GOALS

A. Improve Employee Retention
B. Improve Productivity and Efficiency
C. Improve Intervals
D. Increase Operational Functions and Product Line Within Center
E. Improve Overall Quality
F. Improve Customer Relations

Strategic Goal A addresses our employees and came about because we had major problems with keeping our employees, especially our good ones. We realized that the time involved to hire and train new employees was taking a toll on our ability to accomplish our Mission. We also recognized that a lot of the problems were not within our realm of control; and therefore, we could not solve many of them. As with our discussions on all of our Goals, we came up with solutions that were within our power to address, and identified and assigned Goals that were above our authority to be addressed by our Director.

Strategic Goal A: <u>IMPROVE EMPLOYEE RETENTION</u>

Goal	Improve Employee Retention
Priority	2
Scope	Develop positive reasons and minimize/eliminate negatives to insure that employees remain within our organization

Target Date	On-Going
Project Lead(s)	All Managers
Current Status	Starting March
Cost (if any)	None known at this time
Impact Statement	If employee retention does not improve, it will decrease expertise, productivity, quality, morale; and customer service will suffer
% to Completion	70%
Approval	Wayne Hernandez

Strategic Goal B addresses both our customers by improving our delivery times and our stockholders by saving money. This Goal also addresses our value discipline because we will utilize operationally excellent principles to address our Tactical Goals and Projects. This Goal was developed to set in motion our continuous improvement philosophy.

Strategic Goal B: <u>IMPROVE PRODUCTIVITY AND EFFICIENCY</u>

Goal	Improve our center's ability to process orders in an efficient manner
Priority	1
Scope	We want to set a standard of continuous improvement in our processes and procedures
Target Date	On-Going
Project Lead(s)	All Managers & Supervisors
Current Status	On-Going
Cost (if any)	None known at this time
Impact Statement	Negative Impact – Potential loss of market share and customer satisfaction Positive Impact – Increase market share and LSD (Local Service Delivery) Sugarland Center growth
% to Completion	Starting March
Approval	Wayne Hernandez

Strategic Goal C addresses our customers by improving each of the intervals involved in delivering our end product to our internal and external customers. It also addresses our stockholders by improving the time to market, improving our billing. We know that improving each interval within our end-to-end process will make a big impact on our Mission. We really bettered this Goal and modified it along with all other interval Goals every month or so because we continually bettered each of them. Our overall Goal went down to less than 15 days from grater than 36. You will see that in a later chapter.

Strategic Goal C: <u>IMPROVE INTERVALS</u>

Goal	Improve overall delivery intervals by 30% over the next three years
Priority	1
Scope	Our overall intervals are running around 37 days We need to utilize operationally excellent process improvements to drop this to less than 26 days
Target Date	3 years
Project Lead(s)	All Managers & Supervisors
Current Status	All measurements have been cut at least in half since start of Goal Some, such as provisioning intervals, have been cut from 17 days to five days Although this Goal has been more than achieved, we still want to continue improvements to our measurements This will insure that our Mission is being accomplished and improved upon
Cost (if any)	Minimal overtime
Impact Statement	Positive Impact – Increase both internal and external customer satisfaction, and Center's operations, and increased income from quicker installation and subsequent billing
% to Completion	100%
Approval	Wayne Hernandez

Strategic Goal D addresses our employees. You may ask how improving functions and product line addresses our employees. This Goal developed from feedback from our employees concerning rumors that occurred every November that our department would be disbanded. The managers believed that this was having a major impact on morale and needed to be addressed in our plan. We had no direct control over what product line we produced or whether or not we increased the number and volume of our existing functions. We knew that we needed to do the things that would put us in a position to take on new functions and/or new product lines. When the question arose as to whether or not we could take on these functions, there was never any doubt in anyone's mind, be it management or line employees everyone welcomed the opportunity. When the opportunity arose, we took on the additional work with minimal impact on our customers or employees because we had planned well ahead of time. We felt that by taking on as much work as possible, and doing it better than anyone else, with continued improvement we would stop the rumors and secure our jobs. It worked well for a couple of years; but once the company declared bankruptcy, upper management in their typical decision-making process, only looked at keeping those organizations in company-owned buildings versus rental. Had they looked at the bottom line, they would have kept the Sugarland department, even if they had to keep the buildings of the three remaining CLEC departments empty. (You will see why I come to this conclusion when we go into the resulting savings for Sugarland verses the other two remaining CLEC departments)

Strategic Goal D: <u>INCREASE OPERATIONAL FUNCTIONS AND PRODUCT LINE WITHIN CENTER</u>

Goal	Increase operational functions and product lines within Sugarland Center
Priority	3
Scope	Pursue/increase ownership for all aspects of long distance and local service for the Local Exchange Carrier's within market segments assigned
Target Date	2 Years
Project Lead(s)	Sr. Manager/Upper Management
Current Status	Have taken ownership of all orders and operations of 2 of the 4 CLEC centers within the company (NOTE: The company now saves major dollars because they now need only half of the employees to do the same amount of work as before we started MissionWon™)
Cost (if any)	Will save the company by consolidating centers
Impact Statement	Ensures long-term stability for the Center Improves internal customer satisfaction with the one-stop shop
% to Completion	50%
Approval	Wayne Hernandez

Strategic Goal E addresses our internal and external customers by providing them with a better product. Although we turned out a good product, there is always room for improvement. Remember in <u>Good to Great</u>, Jim Collins says, "Good is the Enemy of Great" because once companies become good, they very seldom put in the extra effort to become great! Our Goal was to become great. Once you finish reading this book, you will see that we accomplished this Goal. We were a GREAT organization!

Through this Strategic Goal E, we developed ways to improve our quality to the point where every member of one team got 100% quality for 12 consecutive months. This team also set the standards for the company in all of our intervals. They took enormous pride in continuing to improve these standards. During this timeframe we increased the number of items we checked along with our sample size from 10, which was about one-third, to all orders.

Strategic Goal E: <u>IMPROVE OVERALL QUALITY</u>

Goal	Improve overall quality of our end product to both our internal and external customers
Priority	2
Scope	Improve overall quality of the orders end-to-end process, both internally and externally to our Center Today's quality is acceptable, but can be improved
Target Date	2 to 3 years
Project Lead(s)	Julia, Mario, all managers & supervisors
Current Status	Order Entry has instituted a buddy check prior to order being sent to Provisioning Quality jumped 1-2 points Provisioning has completed the pilot in Mario's city team with 0 errors for the past 6 months Mario is assisting all other city teams implementing the process
Cost (if any)	None
Impact Statement	Positive Impact - Increase productivity, intervals, internal customer satisfaction, and morale
% to Completion	95%
Approval	Wayne Hernandez

Strategic Goal F addresses our customers. It was mostly developed to improve our relationships with our internal customers, but we also looked for opportunities to improve our external customer relationships. Prior to implementing this Goal, we had fairly good relationships with our internal customers; but we felt that if we nurtured these relationships, we could make significant improvements that could impact many of our other Goals. Initially this Goal took a turn for the worst due to the impact of our other Goal of improving intervals. As a bi-product of improving the intervals that we provided our end customer's service, we pushed pretty hard on our internal customers who were not receptive to the additional pressure. Once they understood why we were pushing them so hard and started seeing the results of both their and our efforts they were extremely pleased with the improvements. I got a call from one of their Directors about six months after we started our push on intervals. She said that she was not a happy camper at first because we were pointing out where they were not doing their jobs as well as they could have been. Now her staff was constantly on their toes and getting their jobs done with much more efficiency. She no longer had to get into their day-to-day business because they were taking care of it. She thanked me and sent my staff a Christmas gift for all their assistance. She also sent each member of the team that handled her orders a gift certificate to a restaurant in Houston. Her Sr. Manager also sent a gift basket to them. This was not our only customer who sent Christmas gifts to our center. Every team in the center got gift baskets at least once a year. This made them work even harder to come up with better ways to work with their customers. This Goal also got us more work as on two occasions I got calls from a Vice-President and a Director asking me if we could take on major customer projects even though they were not assigned to us as end customers. They explained that the project was extremely important and their customers had both no tolerance for mistakes or delays. From past experiences with our center, they felt that we were the best center in the company to handle these critical projects. Although we had our normal work that had to be done, my managers, supervisors, and entire staff, said they wanted the opportunity to step up. Just as they always did, in both cases they got the project done on time with no problems. Both our internal and external customers were extremely pleased with the results.

Strategic Goal F: <u>IMPROVE CUSTOMER RELATIONSHIPS</u>

Goal	Improve customer relationships
Priority	2
Scope	Improve both internal and external customer communications and interactions By taking ownership of the orders from end-to-end, we will not make friends with our internal customers In order to overcome, we must be proactive in all other areas such as communicating to them why we push them to move the orders along
Target Date	On-Going
Project Lead(s)	Julia, Amar, and Entire Organization

Current Status	All employees are aware of this Goal and actively practicing improving their daily interaction with IE's The IE training program by Julia and the OE (Order Entry) team has been completed, and all of the IE (Implementation Engineers) managers and their teams have completed this program The Provisioning team's IE training program is complete, and two IE teams have been through the program by Amar
Cost (if any)	A BIG Smile
Impact Statement	Positive Impact – Decrease our intervals and improve customer satisfaction
Negative Impact	Lack of internal customer support and loss of external customer base
% to Completion	90%
Approval	Wayne Hernandez

Below is the Mission Statement for a small network service company along with the Strategic Goals that we developed to accomplish their Mission. This company's goal was to increase the engineering services side of their business to balance out their hardware sales. We, therefore, focused our plan around customer intimate value disciplines. And since we wanted to focus the company on engineering services, many of the Goals developed came from David H. Maister's <u>Managing The Professional Service Firm</u>. Notice the differences in the Strategic Goals between the two companies. As you go into the later chapters you will also notice the differences in the Tactical Goals and the Projects in the two companies. Remember one company focuses on being an operationally excellent company, and the other focuses on being customer intimate.

The only problem with the implementation of this plan was that the Vice-President of Sales, who was also one of the owners, decided not to participate in development or even buy into the final plan once it was developed. He also refused to allow his sales team to work in conjunction with the engineering team as they did the things they needed to do to accomplish their Goals. Just as it is extremely difficult for a basketball team to win if they don't play together as a team, it is just as difficult to succeed if the sales team is not working with the engineers who are implementing the products they sell. In spite of the constant conflict, some of the Goals were completed and many were being implemented. After I left the company, the new Vice-President asked my managers what they were doing. They gave him a copy of the

MissionWon™ plan that we developed. He read it and told them that was exactly what they should be doing and to keep it up. We will go into the results later, but once the flywheel effect kicked in, the company tripled in volume in a two-year period.

> **MISSION - "To Deliver Outstanding Customer Service Through Customer Intimate Value Disciplines, to Provide Fulfilling Careers and Professional Satisfaction to Our Employees, and to Achieve Financial Success Through Growth and Productivity"**

STRATEGIC GOALS

    A. Improve Productivity
    B. Raise Client Satisfaction
    C. Improve Profitability
    D. Increase Skill Building and Dissemination of Skills
    E. Attain Cisco Gold Status
    F. Get Better Business
    G. Increase Services Sales

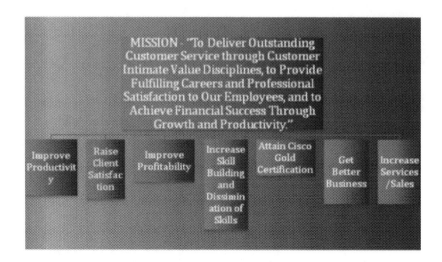

Strategic Goal A: <u>IMPROVE PRODUCTIVITY</u>

Goal	Improve employee productivity
Priority	2
Scope	Improve employee productivity of all employees
Target Date	On-Going
Project Lead(s)	Lonnie, Dorsey
Current Status	In beginning stages
Cost (if any)	N/A
Impact Statement	Positive Impact – Improved resource utilization Fewer employees need to be hired to accomplish workload
Negative Impact	Will cost the company money if we have to hire more employees than we need
% to Completion	10%
Approval	Wayne Hernandez

Strategic Goal B: <u>RAISE CLIENT SATISFACTION</u>

Goal	Raise our client's satisfaction with our services and products
Priority	1
Scope	Raise our clients' satisfaction by utilizing customer intimate value disciplines, i.e., nurturing our customers

Target Date	On Going
Project Lead(s)	Lonnie, Dorsey, Blake
Current Status	Training engineers in technical and customer-intimate principles
Cost (if any)	$100,000 to be shared with Cisco Gold Strategic Goal
Impact Statement	Positive Impact - Improved customer satisfaction and improve our ability to keep our customers along with their repeat services and replacement business
% to Completion	20%
Approval	Wayne Hernandez

Strategic Goal C: <u>IMPROVE PROFITABILITY</u>

Goal	Improve company's profits
Priority	1
Scope	Improve company's profits by improving certifications of the company and engineers, increasing profit margins, increasing/upgrading customer base, expanding operations, etc.
Target Date	On-Going
Project Lead(s)	Wayne
Current Status	Cisco Gold achieved, sales working on higher level customer base, Jackson office opened, and Houston office in Project stage
Cost (if any)	$550,000 per year in salaries, training, and overhead
Impact Statement	Continued improvement to company bottom line Failure to improve profits will negatively impact the company in many ways; such as ability to service our customers, limit growth, and minimize our ability to provide training and financial rewards to our employees
% to Completion	35%
Approval	Wayne Hernandez

Strategic Goal D: <u>INCREASE SKILL BUILDING AND DISSIMINATION OF SKILLS</u>

Goal	Increase employee's skills and sharing of skills of

	more experienced employees
Priority	1
Scope	Improve skill levels of all employees through training and sharing of skills and experience among employees
Target Date	On-Going
Project Lead(s)	Wayne, Lonnie, Dorsey
Current Status	Engineers are being assigned as a team when possible with a more experienced team leader and a younger engineer Engineers with special training and skills are holding training classes for other engineers
Cost (if any)	None
Impact Statement	Improve training and speed of educating employees at no cost
% to Completion	65%
Approval	Wayne Hernandez

Strategic Goal E: <u>ATTAIN CISCO GOLD STATUS</u>

Goal	Attain Cisco Gold Certification
Priority	1
Scope	Commit appropriate financial resources and training required to complete Cisco Gold certification requirements
Target Date	7 months
Project Lead(s)	Wayne
Current Status	Completed within 7-month Goal on first attempt
Cost (if any)	$135,000 in training and lab equipment
Impact Statement	Improved status in industry, increased profit margin, increased services, improved relationship with main vendor resulting in increased training and sales opportunities
% to Completion	100 %
Approval	Wayne Hernandez

Strategic Goal F: <u>GET BETTER BUSINESS</u>

Goal	Improve our customer base by focusing on larger customers and a larger percentage of their business We need to better communicate with our

	customers and focus on long-term relationships
Priority	2
Scope	Sales team to focus on larger businesses with larger networks and financial backing
Target Date	On going
Project Lead(s)	Wayne, Charles
Current Status	The main Hospital Service Company in the US has committed to use us for all services throughout US The sales team is working on bringing on mid-sized telecommunications companies as new customers
Cost (if any)	None
Impact Statement	Increased profits, long-term company stability
% to Completion	20 %
Approval	Wayne Hernandez

7

TACTICAL GOALS

"Nothing is more harmful to the service, than the neglect of discipline; for that discipline, more than numbers, gives one army superiority over another."

George Washington

MissionWon™ meets the above statement because it builds discipline within the company or organization, giving it superiority over its competition.

Now that we have identified our Strategic Goals, we move into the phase of developing the Tactical Goals. In the process of completing these Tactical Goals, our Strategic Goals are being addressed.

Just as in typical Tactical Plans, the time frame for our Goals is shorter than our Strategic Goals' timeframe, typically one to three years in length. These Goals should be more detailed than our Strategic Goals and more detailed in scope. Tactical Goals should be well thought out and address the Strategic Goal in more specificity. These Tactical Goals should be developed in working sessions of the lower levels of managers that participated in the Strategic Goal session and at least their management level subordinates. In larger organizations, the next level of management may also be involved in these working sessions. A facilitator should also be assigned to moderate these sessions to insure structure and adherence to the process. There can be as many Tactical Goals as necessary to insure that the Strategic Goal will be accomplished. There must be at least one Tactical Goal for each Strategic Goal. In reality, you should have a number of Tactical Goals for each.

Remember, in discussions on these Tactical Goals, managers should always take into consideration the value disciplines that were previously decided upon. This means that the majority of these Tactical Goals will be designed around that value discipline, although there will still be Goals developed around some of the other value disciplines. Remember we still have to meet minimal standards in the two other values. Just as important, we need to discuss the problems that we are experiencing or anticipate experiencing in the future. In discussing these problems, we will also discuss possible tactical solutions. The solutions that are ultimately agreed upon will be translated into our Tactical Goals. Remember at this level we are working at tactical levels and the details will be worked out in the Project Goal sessions. This is also an important phase since we are working on setting the direction for our future Project sessions.

Let's look at what information we need to identify in our sessions for each of these Tactical Goals. As you can see, they are the same as we have for our Strategic Goals.

- GOAL: A general description of the Tactical Goal.
- PRIORITY: Rank the Goal on the basis of importance in relation to other Tactical Goals. If its Strategic Goal is a priority one, then the majority of the Tactical Goals' priorities that fall under it should be ones with a few twos and threes at the most. This will insure that we accomplish our Strategic Goal at the priority we established. If the majority of our Tactical Goals are twos and threes, we won't accomplish our Strategic Goal as a one priority. More than one Goal may be assigned the same priority because we will be working on them at the same time.
- SCOPE: The scope must be in enough detail so that anyone in the organization reading it will understand its intent.
- TARGET DATE: These Goals are more specific, they should be at least one to three years in time frame. It is difficult to set a specific Target date for these since they are still fairly long in range but should be a little closer than our Strategic Goal dates. This date can either be estimated start dates or completion dates, but they must remain consistent. Either this date is your estimated start date or your estimated complete date. If desired, both the estimated start and completion dates can be used. Remember this is a working document and these dates can be changed so make your best estimate. You may also want to identify a quarter such as "third quarter of 20XX."

- PROJECT LEAD(S): This should be the Project leader or person or persons responsible to insure that this Goal is accomplished. Since this is a mid-level Goal, it should be assigned to a mid-level manager with the authority to insure that the Tactical Goals and in particular the Projects are accomplished. It may be that the majority of the Project Managers are members of his organization. This would insure that they have not only the responsibility, but also the authority to make sure that progress is being made on these Goals. You may even want to assign this to a group of managers or supervisors depending on the size of the organization, i.e., all first line managers.
- CURRENT STATUS: This should be a roll up from the current status of all of the Project Goals that feed this Tactical Goal.
- COST (if any): This is a best guess of the total costs of the Projects that feed this Goal.
- IMPACT STATEMENT: This statement will identify any impact either positive, negative, or both, that this Goal will have on our Mission. Example, if this Goal is not accomplished by July of 20XX, we will be forced to hire contract employees. Example, if we accomplish this Goal by July of 20XX we will be able to expand our markets without additional expenses. Example, if we continue to raise our customers' expectations, our competitors will have a hard time to catch up to our standards.
- % TO COMPLETION: This is the average of the % To Completion of the Project Goals that feed this Tactical Goal. Although this is never perfectly accurate, it will give upper management a good estimate of where they stand in respect to accomplishing their Tactical Goals.
- APPROVED BY: This would be the name of the Manager(s) or Supervisor(s) who approved the Goal, along with the date of initial approval or the date of approval of modifications.

Let's look again at our Mission Statements and then the Tactical Goals that feed the Strategic Goals that were generated to guide our accomplishments. Here is our Mission Statement for the telecommunication company's CLEC department.

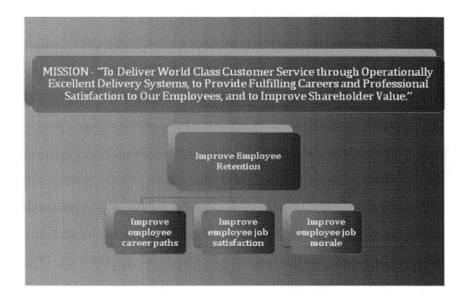

MISSION - "To Deliver World Class Customer Service through Operationally Excellent Delivery Systems, to Provide Fulfilling Careers and Professional Satisfaction to Our Employees, and to Improve Shareholder Value."

Strategic Goal A: <u>IMPROVE EMPLOYEE RETENTION</u>

Tactical Goal A1: <u>Improve employee career paths</u>

Scope	Improve career paths for our employees Align job duties with pay grades to provide a more consistent career path strategy with competitive salaries - 80% to midpoint
Priority	2
Target Date	2nd Qtr 20XX

Project Lead(s)	Sr. Mgr/Mgrs
Current Status	Employees in study phase Results due by end of 1st quarter
Cost (if any)	Not known at this time
Impact Statement	By doing this we will provide consistency and direction in our employees careers
% to Completion	20%
Approved by	Amar, Sandra, Andy, Art, Harvey, Justin

Tactical Goal A2: Improve employee job satisfaction

Scope	To continue to increase employee's level of job satisfaction based on employee surveys
Priority	2
Target Date	Ongoing
Project Lead(s)	All Managers
Current Status	In process
Cost (if any)	None
Impact Statement	Will improve morale and help retain employees In discussions with employees, they are happy with local management, but not with corporate level management By addressing the surveys we can hopefully improve
% to Completion	Ongoing
Approved by	Amar, Sandra, Andy, Art, Harvey, Justin

Tactical Goal A3: Improve employee job morale

Scope	Continue to improve employee morale
Priority	1
Target Date	Ongoing
Project Lead(s)	OE- Julia, Kimberly, Angie, Kenya, Doris/LSA (Local Service Access) Mgrs
Current Status	Ongoing
Cost (if any)	Minimal
Impact Statement	By continuing to improve morale, we will continue to provide the best customer service
% to Completion	Ongoing
Approved by	Amar, Sandra, Andy, Art, Harvey, Justin

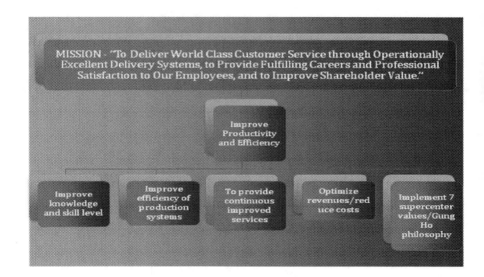

Strategic Goal B:
IMPROVE PRODUCTIVITY
AND EFFICIENCY

Tactical Goal B1: Improve knowledge and skill level

Scope	Better educate our employees in all aspects of their jobs
Priority	1
Target Date	Ongoing
Project Lead(s)	OE- Julia /LSD Mgrs
Current Status	OE Manager has met with each individual/Supervisor to assess current skill sets and opportunities for improvement LSA Managers in process of meetings
Cost (if any)	Minimal
Impact Statement	Continuing improvement in quality and throughput
% to Completion	25%
Approved by	Amar, Sandra, Andy, Art, Harvey, Justin

Tactical Goal B2: Improve efficiency of production systems (enhance activation and other service delivery processes to support increased growth and optimize revenues)

Scope	Actively participate in enhancement

	recommendations and testing of new systems and enhancements to existing ones
Priority	2
Target Date	Ongoing
Project Lead(s)	All Managers
Current Status	Ongoing
Cost (if any)	Unknown
Impact Statement	Improved throughput of all processes
% to Completion	25%
Approved by	Amar, Sandra, Andy, Art, Harvey, Justin

Tactical Goal B3: <u>To Provide Continuous Improved Services To Our Customers</u>

Scope	To improve all of our services to our customers
Priority	1
Target Date	4th Qtr
Project Lead(s)	All Managers/Supervisors
Current Status	Ongoing
Cost (if any)	Unknown
Impact Statement	Improved intervals/better products
% To Completion	20%
Approved by	Amar, Sandra, Andy, Art, Harvey, Justin

Tactical Goal B4: Optimize revenues/reduce costs

Scope	To ensure that we provide our services with minimum costs and optimize our customer revenue
Target Date	Ongoing
Project Lead(s)	All Manager/Supervisors
Current Status	Ongoing
Cost (if any)	None known at this time
Impact Statement	Improved company bottom line
% to Completion	75%
Approved by	Amar, Sandra, Andy, Art, Harvey, Justin

Tactical Goal B5: Implement 7 Super Center values/Gung Ho philosophy

Scope	Roll out Gung Ho values to all employees
Priority	2
Target Date	4th Qtr

Project Lead(s)	OE- Julia
Current Status	Completed
Cost (if any)	None
Impact Statement	Improved employee morale which will result in improved production
% to Completion	100%
Approved by	Amar, Sandra, Andy, Art, Harvey, Justin

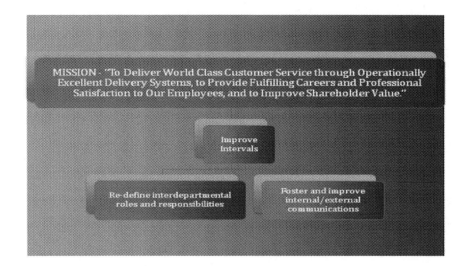

Strategic Goal C: <u>IMPROVE INTERVALS</u>

Tactical Goal C1: Re-define interdepartmental roles and responsibilities

Scope	To look for ways to redefine roles and responsibilities to improve production intervals
Target Date	Ongoing
Project Lead(s)	All Managers and Supervisors
Current Status	On going
Cost (if any)	None Known
Impact Statement	Improved customer service through improved intervals
% to Completion	20%
Approved by	Amar, Sandra, Andy, Art, Harvey, Justin

Tactical Goal C2: <u>Foster and improve internal/external communications</u> (see Tactical Goal F4)

Scope	To encourage and find ways to improve communications
Priority	1
Target Date	4th Qtr
Project Lead(s)	OE- Julia
Current Status	OE-Scheduled Service Advantage class
Cost (if any)	Not Known
Impact Statement	Improved relationships with internal and external customers will lead to improved intervals and improved customer satisfaction
% to Completion	20%
Approved by	Amar, Sandra, Andy, Art, Harvey, Justin

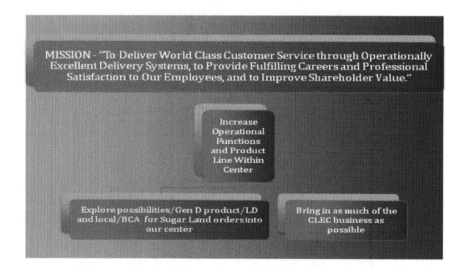

Strategic Goal D: <u>INCREASE OPERATIONAL FUNCTIONS AND PRODUCT LINE WITHIN CENTER</u>

Tactical Goal D1: <u>Explore possibilities/Gen D products/LD (Long distance) and Local/BCA (Business Customer Accounts) for Sugarland orders into our center</u>

Scope	Explore new Gen D product/LD and LEC orders for Sugarland Center (See TG D2)
Priority	3
Target Date	2004

Project Lead(s)	Sr. Manager, Managers
Current Status	Have taken over all LSD orders for former MCI, and Dallas has taken on Gen D orders
Cost (if any)	Additional employees and training
Impact	Increased job security, improved profitability
% to Completion	75%
Approved by	Amar, Sandra, Andy, Art, Harvey, Justin

Tactical Goal D2: <u>Bring in as much of the CLEC Business as possible</u>

Scope	To continue to take on more CLEC volume
Priority	1
Target Date	4th Qtr
Project Lead(s)	Sr. Manager
Current Status	Brought in all Dallas CLEC Dallas Super Center customers and all Fredrick CLEC customers thus tripling the number of orders we process
Cost (if any)	Additional 30 employees
Impact Statement	Ensures long-term stability for the Center Improves internal customer satisfaction by having a one-stop shop for all Major customers
% to Completion	100%
Approved by	Amar, Sandra, Andy, Art, Harvey, Justin

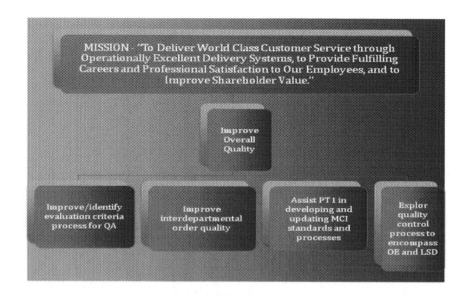

Strategic Goal E: <u>IMPROVE OVERALL QUALITY</u>

Tactical Goal E1: <u>Improve/identify evaluation criteria process for QA</u>
(Quality Assurance)

Scope	Revise QA evaluation process to more accurately reflect changes in the business and eliminate mistakes
Target Date	4th Qtr
Project Lead(s)	OE- Stacie, LSD- Kevin
Current Status	OE-Completed, LSD-Started review
Cost (if any)	None
Impact Statement	Improve quality of service delivered to internal and external customers
% to Completion	100%
Approved by	Amar, Sandra, Andy, Art, Harvey, Justin

Tactical Goal E2: <u>Improve interdepartmental order quality</u>

Scope	Set up process to verify quality prior to sending order to LSD
Priority	1
Target Date	1st Qtr 2002
Project Lead(s)	OE-Betty, Stacie

Current Status	OE- Checking process in place Reports being provided to management
Cost (if any)	None
Impact Statement	Improved quality between OE and LSD. Eliminates orders being sent back to OE
% to Completion	100%
Approved by	Amar, Sandra, Andy, Art, Harvey, Justin

Tactical Goal E3: <u>Assist PTI in developing and updating MCI standards and processes</u>

Scope	Continue to participate in assisting PTI in improvement of standards and processes Projects are developed as needed
Priority	1
Target Date	Ongoing as requested by PTI
Project Lead(s)	All Managers and Supervisors
Current Status	Being done as requested by PTI
Cost (if any)	None
Impact Statement	Improved intervals, improvement in product delivery to customers
% to Completion	Ongoing
Approved by	Amar, Sandra, Andy, Art, Harvey, Justin

Tactical Goal E4: <u>Explore quality control process to encompass OE and LSD</u>

Scope	To develop OE and LSD quality control procedures to catch/eliminate errors prior to orders moving onto the next phase of the process
Priority	1
Target Date	OE: 4th Qtr LSD: 4th Qtr
Project Lead(s)	OE: Julia LSD: Mario
Current Status	OE: Complete LSD: Rolling out to all teams
Cost (if any)	None
Impact Statement	Eliminate mistakes on a proactive basis therefore eliminating delays later in the process
% To Completion	90%
Approved by	Amar, Sandra, Andy, Art, Harvey, Justin

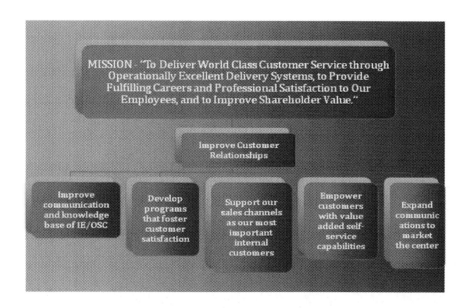

Strategic Goal F: <u>IMPROVE CUSTOMER RELATIONSHIPS</u>

Tactical Goal F1: <u>Improve communication and knowledge base of IE/OSC</u>
(Operations Service Consultant)

Scope	Improve our communication with and knowledge of our internal customers
Priority	1
Target Date	3rd Qtr.
Project Lead(s)	Kathleen, Harvey
Current Status	In development stage
Cost (if any)	None
Impact Statement	Improve our communication with IE's and Operations The more we understand their problems and they understand ours the better we can serve them and our external customers.
% to Completion	5%
Approved by	Amar, Sandra, Andy, Art, Harvey, Justin

Tactical Goal F2: <u>Develop programs that foster customer satisfaction</u>

Scope	We need to institute programs that will help our internal and external customers look at us as the solution to their problems Reset the previous standards that we set in customer satisfaction
Priority	2
Target Date	3rd Qtr
Project Lead(s)	Ron
Current Status	Some of these programs in place at the present time Ron, managers, and supervisors are working toward finding additional ideas
Cost (if any)	None
Impact Statement	Continued positive customer satisfaction
% to Completion	45%
Approved by	Amar, Sandra, Andy, Art, Harvey, Justin

Tactical Goal F3: Support our Sales channels as our most important internal customers (See Tactical Goals: C2, F1, F2, F4)

Scope	Have been doing just this in Sugarland, and the Dallas Super Center has taken it as a Goal We therefore need to refocus our efforts to improve our support to our sales channel
Priority	2
Target Date	Ongoing
Project Lead(s)	All Managers
Current Status	We have already addressed this Goal throughout our plan, but we want to reinforce it
Cost (if any)	None known at this time
Impact Statement	Improved customer satisfaction
% to Completion	85%
Approved by	Amar, Sandra, Andy, Art, Harvey, Justin

Tactical Goal F4: Empower customers with value added self-service capabilities by transitioning information to Dallas Super Center web-based platform (See Tactical Goal C2)

Scope	To better inform our internal customers of our services and ways to improve the sharing of information

Priority	2
Target Date	2nd Qtr
Project Lead(s)	Stephen
Current Status	Initial meetings with data processing
Cost (if any)	Dallas Super Center to support
Impact	Improved support to our internal customers
% To Completion	10%
Approved by	Amar, Sandra, Andy, Art, Harvey, Justin

Tactical Goal F5: <u>Expand communications to market the center</u>

Scope	Need to do a better job of educating the IE and Operations groups of what we do and why we do the things we do to improve our working relationships
Priority	2
Target Date	1st Qtr
Project Lead(s)	Corasha
Current Status	In process
Cost (if any)	None
Impact Statement	Improved working relationships with our internal customers
% to Completion	10%
Approved by	Amar, Sandra, Andy, Art, Harvey, Justin

Let's look at the Mission Statement for the data networking company and then the Tactical Goals that feed the Strategic Goals that were generated to guide their accomplishments. Remember that this company's value discipline is different from the one we just reviewed. They wanted to focus on customer intimacy whereas our telecommunications company focused on being operationally excellent. Notice the differences in the Tactical Goals between the two companies. We won't go into the level of detail in this example that we went into above.

MISSION - "To Deliver Outstanding Customer Service Through Customer Intimate Value Disciplines, to Provide Fulfilling Careers and Professional Satisfaction to Our Employees, and to Achieve Financial Success Through Growth and Productivity"

TACTICAL GOALS

Strategic Goal A	*Improve Productivity*
Tactical Goal A1	Leverage engineer by skill level
Tactical Goal A2	Improve Efficiency
Tactical Goal A3	Improve Project Management Performance
Tactical Goal A4	Improve Business Procedures and Practices
Tactical Goal A5	Formalize our organization
Tactical Goal A6	Improve non billable time
Tactical Goal A7	Document policies and procedures

Strategic Goal B	*Raise Client Satisfaction*
Tactical Goal B1	Improve availability to customers
Tactical Goal B2	Continue to raise customer expectations
Tactical Goal B3	Nurture existing customers
Tactical Goal B4	Listen to customers

Strategic Goal C	*Improve Profitability*
Tactical Goal C1	Lower costs
Tactical Goal C2	Raise prices
Tactical Goal C3	Increase billable hours per engineer
Tactical Goal C4	Increase number of profitable services
Tactical Goal C5	Expand profitable services
Tactical Goal C6	Decrease/phase out non profitable, low profit services

Strategic Goal D	Increase Skill Building and Dissemination of Skills
Tactical Goal D1	Improve employee's experiences
Tactical Goal D2	Orientation for new employees
Tactical Goal D3	Improve employee expertise

Strategic Goal E	Attain Cisco Gold Status
Tactical Goal E1	Hire/certify a minimum of 4 CCIEs (Cisco Certified Internet Expert)
Tactical Goal E2	Hire/certify a minimum of 2 CCDPs (Cisco Data Professional)
Tactical Goal E3	Develop network lab
Tactical Goal E4	Hire/certify 1 CCNP (Cisco Network Professional)
Tactical Goal E5	Develop onsite 4 hr. response w/parts operations
Tactical Goal E6	Develop direct support contract
Tactical Goal E7	Process change to 51% of calls escalated by CCIE's

Strategic Goal F	Get Better Business
Tactical Goal F1	Marketing by experience, education, and superior knowledge
Tactical Goal F2	Focus on customer intimate values
Tactical Goal F3	Look at repackaging services
Tactical Goal F4	Invest in newer higher value services

8

Projects or Changes

"Develop the winning edge; small differences in your performance can lead to large differences in your results."

Brian Tracy

MissionWon™ meets the above statement by developing Projects or Changes that build and lead to large differences which result in the winning edge.

Now that we have identified our Tactical Goals, we move into the phase of crafting the Projects or Changes to our existing policies and procedures to address our Tactical Goals. In the process of completing these Projects or Changes, our Tactical Goals will automatically happen. We can identify as may Projects or Changes in the way we conduct business today as needed to address our Tactical Goals. We want to identify all possible Projects even though we cannot do them today or even this year. We will identify them and put dates as To Be Determined (TBD) and Priority as a five. As our Tactical Goals are being addressed and completed, our Strategic Goals are automatically being addressed. Thus our Mission is accomplished through a disciplined methodology.

Just as in typical project plans, the time frame to complete them is, typically less than a year. These projects will be very specific in detail. Tactical Goals should be well thought out and should address the Strategic Goal in more specificity. These Projects should be developed in working sessions of the lower levels of managers who participated in the Tactical Goal sessions and the line employees who actually do the job functions. It is important that we get input from this level, as they are the ones who can best identify the problems and possible solutions needed to set us on the course of continuous improvement. In larger organizations, the first level of management should also be involved in these working sessions. A facilitator should be assigned to moderate these sessions to insure structure and adherence to the process.

There can be as many Projects, or Changes to processes, and procedures as necessary to insure that the Tactical Goal will be accomplished. There must be at least one Project for each Tactical Goal. In reality, you should have a number of Projects for each.

Remember, in discussions on these Projects, managers should always take into consideration the value disciplines that were previously decided upon. This means that the majority of these Projects will be designed around that value discipline, although there will still be Projects developed around some of the other value disciplines. Remember we still have to meet minimal standards in the two other values. Just as important, we need to discuss the problems that we are experiencing or anticipate experiencing in the future. In discussing these problems, we will also discuss possible solutions. The solutions that are ultimately agreed upon will be translated into our Projects or Changes to our processes and procedures. Remember at this level we are working on specifics. This is an important phase since we will be identifying precisely what and how we are going to accomplish our Mission.

Let's look at what information we need to identify in our sessions for each of these Projects. As you can see, they are much the same as we have for our Strategic and Tactical Goals.

- GOAL: A general description of the Project or Change in our business process.
- PRIORITY: Rank the Project on the basis of importance in relation to other Projects and its Tactical Goal. If its Tactical Goal is a priority one, then the majority of the Projects that fall under that Tactical Goal should be ones and a few twos with maybe a few threes at the most. This will insure that we accomplish our Tactical Goal at the priority we established. If the majority of our Projects are twos and threes, we will not accomplish it as a number one priority. More than one Goal may be assigned the same priority since we will be working on a number of them at the same time.
- SCOPE: The scope must be in enough detail so that anyone in the organization reading it will understand its intent.
- TARGET DATE: These Goals are more specific, the majority should be one year in time frame but some can be longer. This date can either be estimated start dates or complete dates, but must remain consistent. Either this date is your estimated start date or your estimated complete date. Both start and end dates may be used. It is difficult to set a specific Target date for these since they are still fairly long in

range but should be a little closer than our Tactical Goal dates. Remember this is a working document, and these dates can be changed so just make your best estimate. You may also want to identify a quarter such as "third quarter of 20XX."

- PROJECT LEAD (S): This should be the Project leader or person or persons responsible to insure that this Goal is accomplished. Since this is a Project, it should be assigned to a high enough level manager or employee with the authority to insure that this Project is accomplished. It may be that the majority of the Project Managers are members of the above Tactical Goal organization. This would insure that they not only have the responsibility, but also the authority to make sure that progress is being made on these Goals.

- CURRENT STATUS: This should be a roll up from the current status of all of the Project Goals that feed this Tactical Goal. It should include any problems that impact this Project.

- COST (if any): This is a best guess of the total costs of this Project.

- IMPACT STATEMENT: This statement will identify any impact either positive or negative or both that this Project or Process Change will have on the Mission. Example -- If this Project (or Process Change) is not accomplished by July of 20XX, we will be forced to hire contract employees. Example - - If we accomplish this Project by July of 20XX we will be able to expand our markets without additional expenses. Example - - If we continue to raise our customer's expectations, our competitors will have a hard time to catch up to our standards.

- % TO COMPLETION: This is the % To Completion of this Project. Although this may not be perfectly accurate, it will give upper management a good estimate of where they stand in respect to accomplishing their Tactical Goal.

- APPROVED BY: This would be the name of the Manager(s) or Supervisor(s) who approved the Goal along with the date of initial approval or the date of approval of modifications.

Let's look again at our Mission Statements and then the Projects that feed the Strategic and Tactical Goals that were generated to guide our accomplishments. Once again, here is our Mission Statement for the telecommunication company's CLEC department. Note: the numbering sequence is A1/1 where A is the 1st Strategic Goal, 1 is the 1st Tactical Goal for that Strategic Goal A, and / 1 is the 1st Project for Strategic Goal A, Project 1. i.e. B2/3 would be Strategic Goal B, Tactical Goal 2, and Project 3.

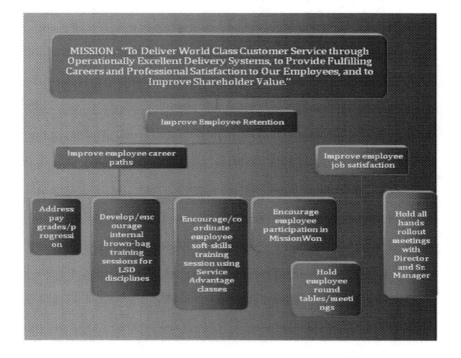

MISSION - "To Deliver World Class Customer Service through Operationally Excellent Delivery Systems, to Provide Fulfilling Careers and Professional Satisfaction to Our Employees, and to Improve Shareholder Value."

A. STRATEGIC GOAL A: Improve Employee Retention

TACTICAL GOAL A1	Improve employee career paths
Project A1/1	Address pay grades/progression

Scope	Align job duties with pay grades to provide a more consistent career path strategy with competitive salaries - 80% to midpoint
Priority	2
Target Date	2nd Qtr
Project Lead(s)	Sr. Mgr/Mgrs
Current Status	Personnel in study phase Results due by end of 1st quarter
Cost (if any)	Not known at this time
Impact Statement	By doing this we will provide consistency and direction to our employees careers
% to Completion	20%
Approved by	All Managers, All Supervisors

Project A1/2	Develop/encourage internal brown-bag training sessions for LSD disciplines
Scope	Develop/encourage internal brown-bag training sessions for LSD disciplines so that employees can educate themselves on the jobs that they seek and better understand the processes
Priority	2
Target Date	1st Qtr 2002 to begin holding classes
Project Lead(s)	LSA- Barbara and Jeanne, OE- Kimberly and Kenya
Current Status	Both LSA and OE brown-bag sessions are being held monthly
Cost (if any)	Cost of 4 Pizza per session. Comes out of Sr. Mgr. Employee satisfaction funds
Impact Statement	Will improve communication within city team and increase employee knowledge
% To Completion	Ongoing
Approved by	All Managers, All Supervisors

Project A1/3	Encourage/coordinate employee soft-skills training session using Service Advantage classes
Scope	Improve customer service skills
Priority	2
Target Date	4th qtr 20XX and 1st qtr 20XX
Project Lead(s)	OE - Julia
Current Status	All OE is scheduled for Nov 12-14, Nov 19-21

	and Dec. 10-12
Cost (if any)	Company sponsored
Impact Statement	Will improve "Customer Service" skills
% To Completion	75%
Approved by	All Managers, All Supervisors

Tactical Goal A2	*Improve employee job satisfaction*
Project A2/1	Hold employee round tables/meetings
Scope	Hold quarterly round tables with all employees
Priority	2
Target Date	Each quarter
Project Lead(s)	OE - Julia / LSD Mgrs
Current Status	Completed for OE, 4th quarter
Cost (if any)	None
Impact Statement	Improve communication between management and staff
% To Completion	15%
Approved by	All Managers, All Supervisors

Project A2/2	Encourage employee participation in Strategic Planning methodology (MissionWon™)
Scope	Provide employees a chance to provide input and participate in action plans to improve the Sugarland organization
Priority	1
Target Date	Ongoing
Project Lead(s)	OE- Julia / LSD Mgrs
Current Status	Ongoing
Cost (if any)	None
Impact Statement	Insure everyone the opportunity to bring his/her ideas for improvement and also the implementation of these ideas
% to Completion	Ongoing
Approved by	All Managers, All Supervisors

Project A2/3	Hold all hands rollout meetings with Director and Sr. Manager
Scope	To improve communication between employees and management

Priority	1
Target Date	Quarterly
Project Lead(s)	Sr. Manager
Current Status	Being held on a quarterly basis
Cost (if any)	$50 per meeting for incidentals
Impact Statement	Improved employee knowledge of management direction
% to Completion	Ongoing

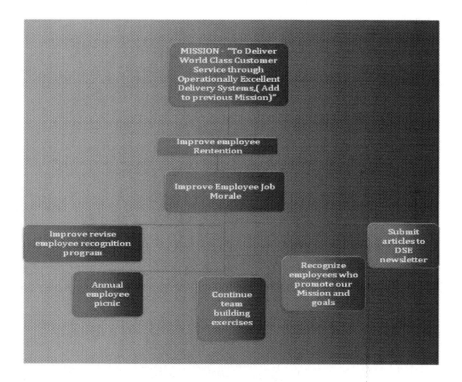

Tactical Goal A3	Improve employee job morale
Project A3/1	Improve/revise employee recognition program
Scope	Continue to make improvements to our recognition of employees
Priority	1
Target Date	Ongoing
Project Lead(s)	LSD- Tammy and Darlene OE - Corasha, Robert

Current Status	Project Leads identified, PFP modified by managers
Cost (if any)	None
Impact Statement	Improvement in employee morale
% to Completion	50%
Approved by	All Managers, All Supervisors

Project A3/2	Annual employee picnic
Scope	Hold annual picnic event for the hub.
Priority	1
Target Date	TBD
Project Lead(s)	LSD - Margaret, Valerie, Denetris, David OE - Kimberlyn, Keesha, Keiwanna
Current Status	Held last year. This year's picnic pending budget allocation information from Super Center
Cost (if any)	TBD
Impact Statement	Strengthen unity and raise overall employee morale
% to Completion	In planning stage
Approved by	All Managers, All Supervisors

Project A3/3	Continue team-building exercises
Scope	Encourage team members to work together as a team
Priority	1
Target Date	Ongoing
Project Lead(s)	All Managers
Current Status	All teams have done off/on site Team Building
Cost (if any)	Picked up by team members
Impact Statement	Improve employee morale and unite team members towards a common Goal
% to Completion	Ongoing
Approved by	All Managers, All Supervisors

Project A3/4	Recognize employees who effectively promote our Mission and Goals via TCB (Technical Consultant Business) Award, Quality Awards, Kudos Awards, Director Award, Sr. Mgr Award, etc.

Scope	Recognize employees for their contributions
Priority	1
Target Date	Ongoing
Project Lead(s)	All Mgrs
Current Status	Ongoing Monthly
Cost (if any)	None, Dallas Super Center picks up cost
Impact Statement	Improved morale and self esteem
% to Completion	Ongoing
Approved by	All Managers, All Supervisors

Project A3/5	Submit articles to Dallas Super Center newsletter (to Anne)
Scope	Promote LSA employee accomplishments
Priority	1
Target Date	Ongoing
Project Lead(s)	Managers and Supervisors
Current Status	Ongoing
Cost (if any)	None
Impact Statement	Improve Sugarland employee visibility throughout Dallas Super Center
% To Completion	Ongoing Monthly
Approved by	All Managers, All Supervisors

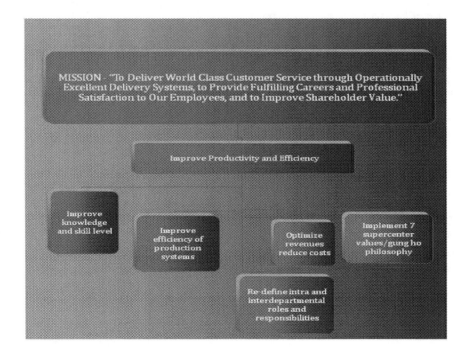

B. *Strategic Goal B: Improve Productivity and Efficiency*

Tactical Goal B1	*Improve knowledge and skill level*
Project B1/1	Create local systems user groups designed to promote individual user proficiency
Scope	Create user groups within the department that can meet/communicate amongst each other their problems and solutions along with best practices
Priority	3
Target Date	4th Qtr.
Project Lead(s)	Kathleen
Current Status	Not started
Cost (if any)	None
Impact Statement	Positive improvement in efficiency, employee moral
% to Completion	0%
Approved by	All Managers, All Supervisors

Project B1/2	Institute OE round table series focusing on LSD

	disciplines (prov/trans/OC)
Scope	Develop quarterly round table discussions on LSD disciplines so that anyone in the OE department can participate
Priority	3
Target Date	1st Qtr
Project Lead(s)	Julia, Angie, Doris
Current Status	Scheduling
Cost (if any)	None
Impact Statement	Improve employee's knowledge of LSD disciplines resulting in improved communication between OE and LSD along with career path knowledge
% to Completion	10%
Approved by	All Managers, All Supervisors

Project B1/3	Develop generic telecom training class through Company University
Scope	Improve employee knowledge of telecommunications
Priority	3
Target Date	4th Qtr
Project Lead(s)	Stephen
Current Status	In process
Cost (if any)	Company sponsored
Impact Statement	Improve employee knowledge
% to Completion	25%
Approved by	All Managers, All Supervisors

Tactical Goal B2	Improve efficiency of production systems
Project B2/1	Integration and familiarization of TPS (Translation Provisioning Software)/CPAS (Circuit Provisioning Access Software)
Goal	To re-visit TPS/CPAS systems and determine how we can utilize them in our process
Project Leads	Barbara, Jeanne and Mario
Current Status	Barbara is working with developers of the system to have it modified so that it will work for Option 2 switches At the present time it only works for Option 1

Cost (if any)	Unknown at this time.
Impact Statement	Will speed up engineering process
% to completion	25%
Approved by	All Managers, All Supervisors

Tactical Goal B3	*Re-define intra and interdepartmental roles and responsibilities*
Project B3/1	Address hours of operation
Scope	Continue to address hours of operation; adjust working hours to better service our customers
Priority	1
Target Date	4th qtr
Project Lead(s)	OE- Julia LSD- Sandra, Amar
Current Status	Completed for OE LSD complete
Cost (if any)	None
Impact Statement	Better customer service since we service all time zones
% to Completion	100%
Approved by	All Managers, All Supervisors

Project B3/2	Move DA (Directory Assistance)/DL (Directory Listings) under one team
Scope	Improve production/efficiency by consolidating all DA/DL listings under Stephen's city team
Target Date	4th qtr
Project Lead(s)	OE - Julia, Kimberly, Kenya, Angie, Doris LSD - Stephen
Current Status	Complete
Cost (if any)	None
Impact Statement	Improved internal and external customer satisfaction
% to Completion	100%
Approved by	All Managers, All Supervisors

Tactical Goal B4	*Optimize revenues/reduce costs*
Project B4/1	Improve CSA (Customer Service Associate) verification process

Scope	TBD
Priority	2
Target Date	Unknown
Project Lead(s)	Unknown
Current Status	Not started at this time
Cost (if any)	Unknown at this time
Impact Statement	Impact to stock holders
% to Completion	0%
Approved by	All Managers, All Supervisors

Project B4/2	Develop/implement process to minimize and reduce expedited charges
Scope	TBD
Priority	1
Target Date	Unknown at this time
Project Lead(s)	Not identified
Current Status	Not started at this time
Cost (if any)	Unknown at this time
Impact Statement	Unknown at this time
% to Completion	0%
Approved by	All Managers, All Supervisors

Project B4/3	Develop/implement process to minimize and reduce supplemental charges
Scope	Work with all LEC's and City Teams to reduce supplemental charges
Priority	2
Target Date	4th Qtr.
Project Lead(s)	Kathleen
Current Status	In initial identification of charges by different LECS
Cost (if any)	None
Impact Statement	Identify ways to reduce the costs incurred when we issue additional charges to the various LEC's
% to Completion	15%
Approved by	All Managers, All Supervisors

Project B4/4	Improve address validation process
Scope	We need to find a better method of verifying

	customer addresses
Priority	3
Target Date	TBD
Project Lead(s)	TBD
Current Status	Need to assign Project Manager
Cost (if any)	Not known at this time
Impact Statement	Positive impact on both time and dollars since matching our records or the field has problems finding sites
% to Completion	0%
Approved by	All Managers, All Supervisors

Tactical Goal B5	Implement 7 Dallas Super Center values/Gung Ho philosophy
Project B5/1	Post values
Scope	Post the center's core values throughout the center
Priority	1
Target Date	4th Qtr
Project Lead(s)	OE- Julia
Current Status	Completed
Cost (if any)	Less than $20
Impact Statement	Insure that our employees are constantly reminded of the center's core values
% to Completion	100%
Approved by	All Managers, All Supervisors

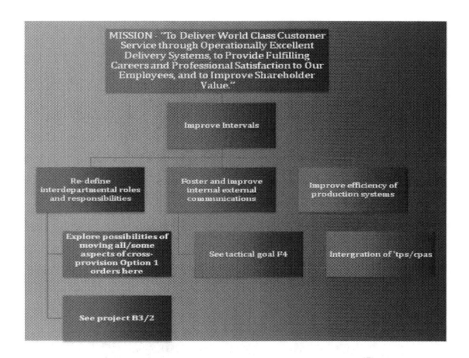

C. *Strategic Goal C: IMPROVE INTERVALS*

Tactical Goal C1	Re-define interdepartmental roles and responsibilities
Project C1/1	Explore possibilities of moving all/some aspects of cross-provision Option 1 orders here
Scope	Streamline the cross-provisioned order process
Priority	4
Target Date	1st Qtr
Project Lead(s)	OE - Angie, LSD - Amar
Current Status	Identifying scope of Project
Cost (if any)	Not known at this time
Impact Statement	Improved cross-provisioned order interval and improved customer satisfaction
% to Completion	10%
Approved by	All Managers, All Supervisors

Project C1/2	See Project B3/2

Tactical Goal C2	Foster and improve internal/external

	communications (see Tactical Goal F4)

Tactical Goal C3	Improved efficiency of production systems
Project C3/1	Integration and familiarization of TPS/CPAS
Scope	Work with company programmers to modify TPS/CPAS to meet our needs
Priority	1
Project Leads	Barbara, Jeanne and Mario
Current Status	Barbara working weekly with TPS/CPAS staff to modify if possible the problems with using this system that was designed for Option 1 to work for our switches At the present time, we cannot use for Option 2
Cost (if any)	Unknown
Impact Statement	Improved productivity
% To completion	15%
Approved by	All Managers, All Supervisors

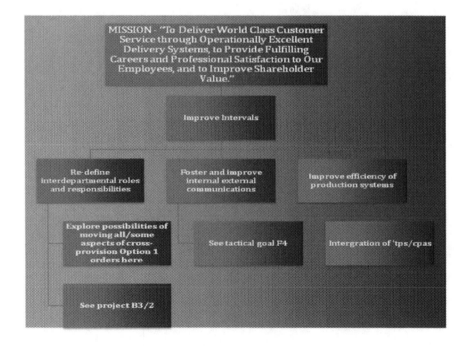

D. Strategic Goal D: *INCREASE OPERATIONAL FUNCTIONS AND PRODUCT LINE WITHIN CENTER*

Tactical Goal D1	*Explore possibilities/Gen d products/LD and Local/BCA for Sugarland orders into our center*
Project D1/1	Form Project team to identify new products and services
Goal	TBD – Since we have just taken over orders from Dallas and Fredrick, this Project is on hold
Priority	4
Target Date	On Hold
Project Lead(s)	Carol
Current Status	On Hold
Cost (if any)	Unknown at this time
Impact Statement	Continue to expand our work to improve our product lines
% to Completion	0%
Approved by	All Managers, All Supervisors

Tactical Goal D2	*Bring in as much of MCI CLEC Business as possible*
Project D2/1	Transition all Dallas CLEC orders to Sugarland
Scope	Take over all LEC orders currently handled by the Dallas Super Center
Priority	1
Target Date	Immediately
Project Lead(s)	Amar
Current Status	Complete
Cost (if any)	15 new employees
Impact Statement	Will free up approximately 130-150 employees in the Dallas Super Center to work on new Gen D products
% to Completion	100%
Approved by	All Managers, All Supervisors

Project D2/2	Transition all Fredrick, MD CLEC orders to Sugarland
Scope	Take over all LEC orders currently handled by

	the Fredrick, MD center
Priority	1
Target Date	Immediately
Project Lead(s)	Amar
Current Status	Complete
Cost (if any)	15 new employees in our office
Impact Statement	Will free up 160 employees in the Fredrick, MD office to work on other products
% To Completion	100%
Approved by	All Managers, All Supervisors

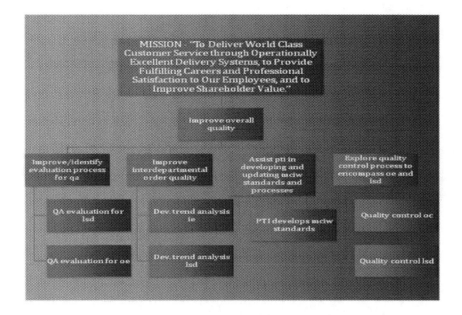

E. *Strategic Goal E: IMPROVE OVERALL QUALITY*

Tactical Goal E1	Improve/identify evaluation process for QA
Project E1/1	Develop new QA evaluation criteria for LSD
Scope	Revise LSD QA evaluation proves to more accurately reflect changes in business and eliminate mistakes
Priority	1
Target Date	1st Qtr
Project Lead(s)	Sandra, Stephen
Current Status	Not assigned – need to assign Project Manager

Cost (if any)	None
Impact Statement	Improve LSD quality of service delivered to internal and external customers
% to Completion	40%
Approved by	All Managers, All Supervisors

Project E1/2	Develop new QA evaluation criteria for OE
Scope	Revise OE QA evaluation proves to more accurately reflect changes in business and eliminate mistakes
Priority	1
Target Date	4th Qtr
Project Lead(s)	Stacie
Current Status	OE- Completed
Cost (if any)	None
Impact Statement	Improve OE quality of service delivered to internal and external customers
% to Completion	100%
Approved by	All Managers, All Supervisors

Tactical Goal E2	*Improve interdepartmental order quality*
Project E2/1	Develop trend analysis to shed light on IE order inconsistencies/inaccuracies on OE side
Scope	Give the IE community information that will assist in identifying specifics related to the rejection of their orders
Priority	2
Target Date	1st Qtr
Project Lead(s)	Corasha
Current Status	In process, in conjunction with Dallas Super Center IE Website development
Cost (if any)	Unknown
Impact Statement	Identification of types of training, which IE's need, to be proactive in eliminating and minimizing delays before the orders get to our office
% to Completion	5%
Approved by	All Managers, All Supervisors

Project E2/2	Trend analysis development to shed light on IE order inconsistencies/inaccuracies on LSD side
Scope	Give the IE community information that will assist them in identifying specifics related to the rejection of their orders by LSD
Priority	3
Target Date	4th Qtr
Project Lead(s)	TBD
Current Status	Need to assign a Project Manager
Cost (if any)	None
Impact Statement	Improve our relationship with internal customers, and improve our order processing
% to Completion	0%
Approved by	All Managers, All Supervisors

Tactical Goal E3	Assist PTI in developing and updating MCI standards and processes
Project E3/1	Assist PTI in developing and updating MCI standards and processes
Scope	Continue to participate in assisting PTI in improvement of standards and processes Projects are developed on an as needed basis when we are requested for assistance We will assign Project Managers
Priority	1
Target Date	On Going
Project Lead(s)	Julia, Sandra
Current Status	Being done as requested.
Cost (if any)	None
Impact Statement	Improved standardization of practices across the company Leaders needed in this effort and take a proactive role
% to Completion	100%
Approved by	All Managers, All Supervisors

Tactical Goal E4	Explore quality control process to encompass OE and LSD
Project E4/1	Develop quality control processes for OE
Scope	To develop OE quality control procedures to

	catch/eliminate errors prior to orders moving onto the next phase of the process
Priority	1
Target Date	4th Qtr
Project Lead(s)	Julia
Current Status	Completed
Cost (if any)	None
Impact Statement	Improved quality by 1-2 points a month giving most employees in this department a monthly bonus
% to Completion	100%
Approved by	All Managers

Project E4/2	Develop quality control processes for LSD
Scope	To develop LSD quality control procedures to catch/eliminate errors prior to orders moving onto the next phase of the process
Priority	1
Target Date	4th Qtr
Project Lead(s)	Mario, Barbara
Current Status	Pilot program extremely successful -- 0 errors for entire team in past 8 months Other LSD teams are in process or rolling out process
Cost (if any)	None
Impact Statement	Eliminate mistakes on a proactive basis, thus eliminating later delays This will grant the majority of LSD staff a monthly bonus
% To Completion	80%
Approved by	All Managers, All Supervisors

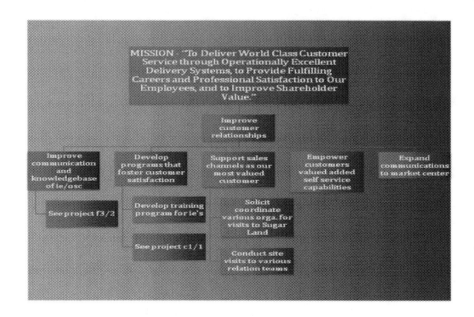

F. Strategic Goal F: IMPROVE CUSTOMER RELATIONSHIPS

Tactical Goal F1	Improve communication and knowledge base of IE/OSC
Project F1/1	See Project F3/2

Tactical Goal F2	Develop programs that foster customer satisfaction
Project F2/1	Develop a training program for IE's
Scope	Develop a training program for the IE so they are familiar with the order process
Priority	2
Target Date	This year
Project Lead(s)	OE-Julia, Corasha
Current Status	In progress
Cost (if any)	None
Impact Statement	Improved customer satisfaction, decrease in orders returned to IE's for additional information
% to Completion	20%
Approved by	All Managers, All Supervisors

Project F2/2	See Project C1/1

Tactical Goal F3	Support our Sales channels as our most important internal customers
Project F3/1	Solicit/coordinate various organizations for familiarization visits to our site (LNET/OSC/IE)
Scope	Encourage our internal customers to visit our offices to improve relationships
Priority	3
Target Date	TBD
Project Lead(s)	Marsha, Mary and Mario
Current Status	On hold due to budget constraints
Cost (if any)	Travel by field
Impact Statement	Improved understanding and communications between our Center and our internal customers
% to Completion	0%
Approved by	All Managers, All Supervisors

Project F3/2	Conduct site visits to various IE/OSC/LEC relations' teams
Scope	To improve relationships with our internal customers by personally visiting them
Priority	2
Target Date	4th Qtr
Project Lead(s)	Sr. Manager and Managers
Current Status	On hold due to budget constraints Have visited all but northeast
Cost (if any)	Approximately $20K
Impact Statement	Form better working relationships with the organizations we deal with on a daily basis
% to Completion	85%
Approved by	All Managers, All Supervisors

Tactical Goal F4	Empower customers with value added self-service capabilities by transitioning information to Dallas Super Center web-based platform

Project F4/1	TBD

Tactical Goal F5	Expand communications to market the center
Project F5/1	TBD

Let's now look at the Projects identified to complete the Mission for the data networking company. Once again we won't go into as much detail as needed in the final plan.

Projects or Changes to the Way We Do Business

MISSION - "To Deliver Outstanding Customer Service Through Customer Intimate Value Disciplines, to Provide Fulfilling Careers and Professional Satisfaction to Our Employees, and to Achieve Financial Success Through Growth and Productivity"

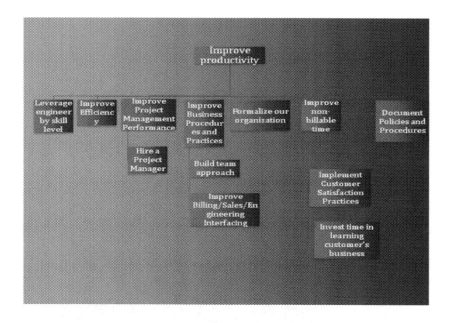

A. Strategic Goal A - Improve Productivity

Tactical Goal A1	Leverage engineer by skill level	
Tactical Goal A2	Improve Efficiency	
Tactical Goal A3	Improve Project Management Performance	
	Project A3/1	Hire a Project Manager
Tactical Goal A4	Improve Business Procedures and Practices	
	Project A4/1	Build team approach
	Project A4/2	Improve Billing/Sales/ Engineering Interfacing
Tactical Goal A5	Formalize our organization	
Tactical Goal	Improve non-	

A6	billable time	
	Project A6/1	Implement Customer Satisfaction Practices
	Project A6/2	Invest time in learning customer's business
Tactical Goal A7	Document Policies and Procedures	

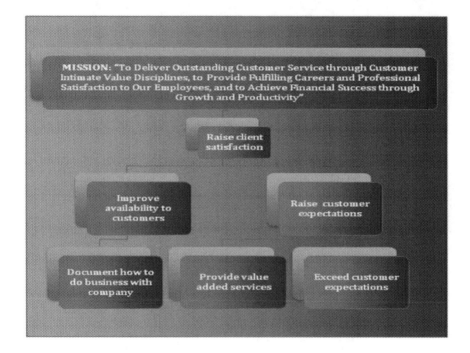

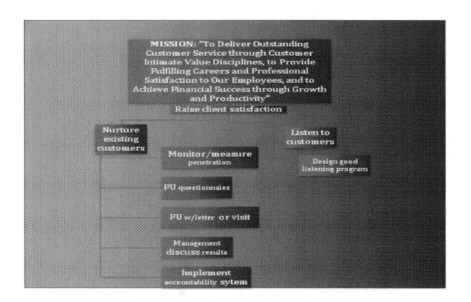

B. *Strategic Goal B - Raise Client Satisfaction*

Tactical Goal B1	Improve availability to customers	
	Project B1/1	Document "How to do Business With Company"
Tactical Goal B2	Continue to raise customer expectations	
	Project B2/1	Continue to provide "value added services" through: (see below)
		Understanding what is "unique" about our customer – what makes each customer different and stand apart
		Pay attention to what he says and what he would like rather than what we desire for him
		Offer first class explanations for what we are doing and why we are doing it
		Assist the customer in understanding what is going on and help him reach

		his own conclusion, not ours
		Keep him adequately educated
		Document our work activities well
		Stay away from unclear terminology
		Be accessible to customer
		Inform customer quickly of modifications and ask for agreement
		Engage customer at most important phases in Project
		Make customer sense he/she is key to us
		Show interest/be supportive to customer beyond our assigned responsibilities
		Learn to persuade, not assert
		Empower the customer with rationale, not just conclusions
		Engage customer in process -- brainstorm/give him action items
		Assist the customer in utilizing what is delivered
		Present options -- let him decide
		Make reports more meaningful
		Send copies of meetings and project plans if important e-mail the next day
		Make meetings more valuable
	Project B2/2	Exceed customer expectations
Tactical Goal B3	Nurture existing customers	
	Project B3/1	Monitor and measure our penetration
	Project B3/2	Follow up questionnaires on each Project
	Project B3/3	Follow up w/letter/visit
	Project B3/4	Management to discuss results with personnel
	Project B3/5	Implement accountability system
Tactical Goal B4	Listen to customers	
	Project B4/1	Design a good listening program w/(see below)

		User Groups
		Reverse seminars
		Attend customer industry meetings
		Market research
		Project team de-briefings

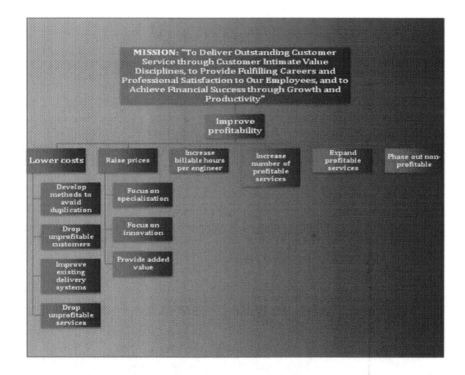

C. Strategic Goal C - Improve Profitability

Tactical Goal C1	Lower costs	
	Project C1/1	Develop methods to avoid duplication
	Project C1/2	Drop unprofitable customers
	Project C1/3	Improve existing delivery systems
	Project C1/4	Drop unprofitable services
Tactical Goal C2	Raise prices	
	Project C2/1	Focus on specialization

	Project C2/2	Focus on innovation
	Project C2/3	Provide added value
Tactical Goal C3	Increase billable hours per engineer	
Tactical Goal C4	Increase number of profitable services	
Tactical Goal C5	Expand profitable services	
Tactical Goal C6	Decrease and phase out non —profitable, low profit services	

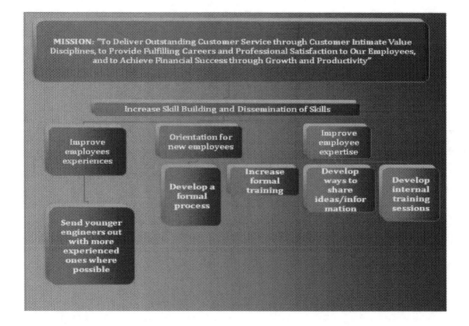

D. *Strategic Goal D - Increase Skill Building and Dissemination of Skills*

Tactical Goal D1	Improve employees experiences	
	Project D1/1	Send younger engineers out with more experienced ones whenever possible
Tactical Goal D2	Orientation for new employees	

	Project D2/1	Develop a formal process
Tactical Goal D3	Improve employee expertise	
	Project D3/1	Increase formal training
	Project D3/2	Develop ways to share ideas/information
	Project D3/3	Develop internal training sessions

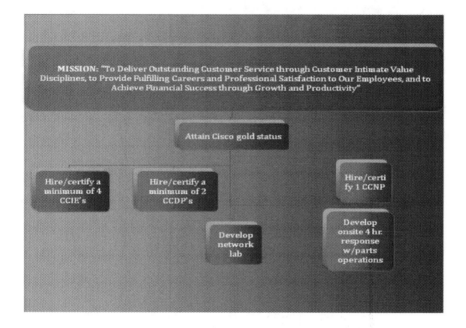

E. Strategic Goal E - Attain Cisco Gold Status

Tactical Goal E1	Hire/certify a minimum of 4 CCIE's	
Tactical Goal E2	Hire/certify a minimum of 2 CCDP's	
Tactical Goal E3	Develop network lab	
Tactical Goal E4	Hire/certify 1 CCNP	
Tactical Goal E5	Develop onsite 4 hr. response w/parts operations	

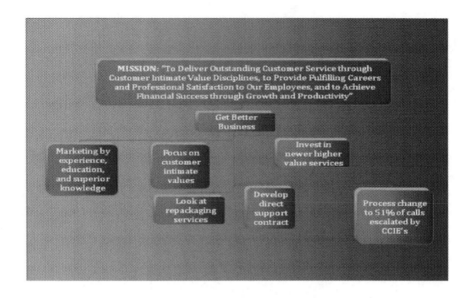

F. *Strategic Goal F - Get Better Business*

Tactical Goal F1	Market by focusing on our experience, education, and superior knowledge	
Tactical Goal F2	Focus on customer intimate values	
Tactical Goal F3	Look at repackaging services	
Tactical Goal F4	Invest in newer higher value services	
Tactical Goal E5	Develop direct support contract	
Tactical Goal E6	Process change to 51% of calls escalated by CCIE's	

9

Goal Approvals

"Most people have the will to win; few have the will to prepare to win."

Bobby Knight

MissionWon™ meets the above statement by providing a road map for all employees to prepare the plan with those who have the desire and will to insure a winning strategy.

The process of approval of the Mission and the Strategic Goals is straight forward as upper management develops them. Since the supervisors and employees who are responsible for performing the daily tasks within the organization develop the Tactical Goals and the Projects, we must have some process so that upper management understands these Goals or Projects. This way they understand how they solve the daily problems and accomplish the higher-level Goals identified through MissionWon™. By having these Goals approved by upper management we accomplish a number of things, such as: eliminate uncertainty, minimize the need for meetings to discuss Projects, focus priorities of the staff, and identify responsibilities, Project Managers, and timeframes for our activities. Manager's meetings are minimized, as not only has the organization's direction been identified, but also the details of how that direction is to be accomplished.

Think about how much time you spend in meetings discussing various Projects that don't even apply to you or your organization. I have spent two to four hours a week in meetings with my bosses discussing details of Projects and problems of my fellow managers because my boss had weekly meetings with all managers. Had everyone implemented MissionWon™, the only topics discussed would have been administrative ones, which could have been accomplished in less than a half hour. The boss would have already discussed and approved most of our Projects and could have reviewed the weekly and monthly reports that are discussed in the following chapter. This way had he had any questions regarding any of the Projects, he could discuss them only with those who are involved and not with his entire staff. The only meetings I had with my immediate staff were those that I called when we had a common problem or something out of the ordinary came up. I did have a monthly meeting with everyone, which lasted about a half hour. In that meeting we announced any monthly or quarterly awards, and I gave them feedback on where we stood on our Goals. As time went on, these meetings became more and more optimistic because our results became more and more positive as the flywheel effect took over. They could see that even though they were putting less effort, the results were coming in at a faster pace and at a level that they never imagined they could achieve.

10

Goal Measuring and Reporting

"Order marches with weighty and measured strides. Disorder is always in a hurry"

Napoleon Bonaparte

MissionWon™ meets the above statement because it builds order with important and measured strides. Therefore it eliminates disorder.

It is important that we measure our Goals to insure that we are making progress towards accomplishing them. Because of the fact that our Strategic and Tactical Goals are accomplished through our Projects, it is not necessary for us to measure each and every one of them. As we accomplish or make progress on any of the Projects, we are automatically making progress on our Tactical Goals. At the same time, since we are making progress on our Tactical Goals, we are automatically making progress on our Strategic Goals. It follows that if we are making progress on our Strategic Goals, we are accomplishing our Mission. We only need to focus tracking our Projects and getting them accomplished. By looking at the structure of MissionWon™, you can see how we cannot help but accomplish our Mission, our Strategic Goals, and our Tactical Goals if we complete our Projects. Therefore, it is most important to track these Projects and insure their successes. We will still track our progress on the higher-level Goals; but not as often or in as much detail unless they are critical to our success, such as our intervals for the telecommunications company. Remember we wanted to be operationally excellent, so getting our orders in and out as quickly and efficiently as possible was extremely important to our continued improvement and ultimate successes.

Another important reason for measuring our progress is the feedback that we can then provide to our employees. I found that by having monthly meetings with all my employees and showing them the monthly, quarterly, and yearly progress they had made, was as big a moral booster as anything else we could have done. We would go over the top 5 to 10 Goals in which we had made the most progress and give out our quality awards. I also created a Sr. Manager award to the one Project Manager or team who made the biggest impact on accomplishing our Goals. That winner or team got use for the month of a scooter that they could use in the office. They were usually too busy to use it, but when they did, their fellow employees would congratulate them by applause as they rode by.

The Project Managers on at least a weekly basis should update the tracking on the MissionWon™ document. Some managers may want this to be updated daily, but this would be a local decision. If the document is located on the company's intranet, it will be the best for not only updating, but also so that everyone in the organization will have access. If not, you may want to assign one person to do all updates so all Project Managers would e-mail their updates to a central site. This person may also be assigned to post the Goals around the work place if you don't have an intranet that all employees can easily access. The assigned managers for the Tactical and Strategic Goals need to look at the updates for all of the Projects or Changes that feed their Goal to determine the status of their assigned Goal. From this they should summarize the status for their Goal. If they see that one or two Goals that feed their Goal are not making progress, then it would be their responsibility to contact the Project Manager or Tactical Goal manager to identify and solve any problems. This makes it easy to monitor, since they get a daily or weekly update and only need to have discussions or meetings if little or no progress is being made or if problems are identified. High-level managers can easily determine the status of all Goals by the % complete and status of each Goal. Should a problem be identified, the upper level manager can pick up a phone or e-mail the Project Manager for answers. Based on the response, he can make appropriate changes such as, changing the priority, or adding resources to get the Goal back on track. Meetings can then be minimized or in some cases eliminated. I had very few manager meetings because I was constantly aware of the status of what was going on in my organization. My boss, David Amador, who was located in Dallas, watched our intervals and backlog reports. As our flywheel effect started to take off, and our numbers got continually better, I only met with him every few months. My daily phone calls (yes, more than one) from him went down to once a week. In that call he would ask me if we were still working there in Houston since he never heard from us and no longer received calls from complaining customers. Since our backlog had been totally eliminated and our numbers were getting better every month, he had no reason to call me every day. As he would say, he had bigger fish to fry. Since our conversations were a lot nicer and much more positive than when I first got on board, I didn't mind talking to him. I have had many bosses in my career and he was one of the best; but let's face it, the less time your boss has to spend talking to you, the more time he has to talk to your fellow managers. The more time he has to talk to them, the more trouble they get into and the less trouble you get into!

11

RESULTS

"Some of us will do our jobs well and some will not, but we will all be judged by only one thing: the result."

Vince Lombardi

MissionWon™ meets the above statement because it insures that the Company's or Organization's Mission is accomplished in a structured environment.

Part of the title of this book says that we will build a disciplined organization culture. I hope by now you can see by the two actual examples, implementing this methodology focuses your entire organization on disciplined thoughts in identifying details required to accomplish your Mission. This can be a Company Mission, a Division Mission, or even down to a Department Mission or lower. Once MissionWon™ is implemented, you will have your entire organization taking disciplined actions by working the Projects or Changes that they identified. Per Mr. Robert Dunham's "Top 14 Mistakes Senior Managers Make" in the preview note of Chapter 1, what we really want is the ownership, pride, and passion that comes where people commit to what they are doing. I think you can now admit that you have disciplined people and a disciplined organization since your people are having disciplined thoughts and taking disciplined actions.

Amar, one of my managers came into my office one day with a big smile on his face. As he leaned his back on my board and crossed his legs and said, "Wayne, it's working!" I was caught off guard and responded, "What's working, Amar?" He said that our planning methodology (MissionWon™) had changed everything. Before we implemented it, he said he used to walk down the rows of his team and had to continually get after them because they were always behind on their orders. He had to continually push them because they had little or no incentive. They could never catch up. Now, he said as he walks down the aisles, his employees are on the phone pushing the field people to get their work completed and turned in timely. They were now focused on getting our customers up and running on our services versus our competitor's! He said that he no longer wasted his time cracking a whip, but solved the few problems that came up and was proactive and taking on many of the Projects that we identified. He said he and most of his staff hated to come to work before, but now they couldn't wait to come in to continue resetting the standards they were setting.

The President of this company on her yearly conference call made reference to successful departments sharing their best practices with other departments. She then suggested if a department had the best provisioning intervals in the company that they should share their methods with the other provisioning teams. You'd be surprised at how fast my managers ran into my office with the biggest smiles on their faces saying, "Did you hear her, she was talking about us!" Within a few weeks I got a call from the Sr. Vice-President's office asking if he could send someone to see how we operated. Of course I said, "Yes." He sent one of his assistant managers in for a couple of days to talk to my managers, my supervisors and me. I think he was looking for one or two big things that he could take back and roll out to the other centers. Sorry, but it wasn't that easy. We did hundreds of little things that amounted to significant results in all areas. Unfortunately, he couldn't just pick one or two to take with him. We had "DISIPLINED PEOPLE THINKING DISIPLINED THOUGHTS and TAKING DISIPLINED ACTIONS." As my managers would say, "They (our upper management) just don't get it!"

Our Vice-President asked each of his 22 Sr. Managers to send him their top five accomplishments for the past year, so I picked out our top five and e-mailed them to him. At his awards banquet, he announced the Super Center's Yearly Top 10 Accomplishments. Yes, you guessed it; five of his Top 10 Accomplishments for the past year were the five that I had sent him! The 130 Sugarland CLEC employees who had disciplined thoughts and took disciplined actions were responsible for one half of the Super Center's accomplishments! That was quite an accomplishment for 130 people when you consider the fact that the Center had about 3,000 employees. Think about it, less than 5% of the employees contributed to 50% of the accomplishments for the entire year. Remember we had "DISIPLINED PEOPLE THINKING DISIPLINED THOUGHTS and TAKING DISIPLINED ACTIONS." No, upper management still "didn't get it."

Remember you won't see the results in a week or even a month, but you will see that flywheel effect. It takes a lot of effort in the beginning to get started, but as more and more Projects start to impact the Mission, the easier and faster the results are seen. Once the results start, less and less effort results in more and more positive impact to all facets of the business. Let's now look at some of our actual Goals and the results. Most of these were achieved within a two-year timeframe. Remember, Here is our Mission Statement.

> **MISSION - "To Deliver World Class Customer Service through Operationally Excellent Delivery Systems, to Provide Fulfilling Careers and Professional Satisfaction to Our Employees, and to Improve Shareholder Value."**

One of our Strategic Goals was to "Improve Overall Quality." We identified a number of Projects that would result in achieving this Goal. Within a two-year period, our quality went from a 97% up to a 99.7% while at the same time tripling order volume and significantly decreasing all of our timeframes. We addressed both our internal and external customers by providing them with services that were pretty close to being perfect and continuing to improve.

Another of our Goals was to "Improve productivity and efficiency." As a result of this Goal, we were able to reduce our "over 60 day old orders" from 65 down to zero. Once we eliminated all of our 60-day-old orders we concentrated on our 45-day-old backlog. We also were able to reduce our "over 45 day old orders" from 110 orders (this number does not include over 400 additional orders we inherited from the other two centers, which we also got down to zero) down to zero. By not holding a backlog of overage orders, we accomplished two parts of our Mission; 1) we addressed our external customers by delivering their service in a timely fashion, and 2) we addressed our stock holders with additional income due to the additional billing we achieved by removing our competitor's services and replacing them with ours 20 days sooner. Our internal customers who dealt with our external customers directly were also happier since they were able to provide service to their customers much sooner and with fewer problems.

We would have three to four hour conference calls every day with managers throughout the company to discuss these backlogged orders. We spent much of our time on these calls that had been instituted at the Sr. Vice-President level. Talk about a big problem with time management. Yes, they were important because we weren't working our orders in a timely manner. But that was the problem: We were not working our orders in a timely manner! Not that we were on conference calls much of the day. Many managers would have seen the conference calls as the problem and tried to address them as the problem by canceling the calls or just not attending them. Since the problem was not working our orders in a timely manner, we identified the changes that we needed to do to make sure we had no orders over 60 days. It took us a little over a year to do it; but guess what, every monthly report showed a zero for our entire over 60-day-old orders. We then started addressing our over 45-day-old orders on these calls. We soon got these down to zero also. None of our managers got on any of these conference calls after that. The other four CLEC teams continued on with the calls. This eliminated a lot of our managers' time being wasted sitting in conference calls listening to the other Center's orders and not ours. Even after we took over the large backlog of orders from the two centers, in a short time we got their backlog down to zero also. How did we eliminate the over-60, -45 and -30 day old orders? Well, there were a number of things that we did, but one of them was to start a report that showed orders that were over 15 days and over 20 days old. Then our managers and supervisors became proactive in addressing the problems that were either holding up an order or anticipated problems that could keep it from being worked on its due date. At 15 days the supervisors started to make sure that everyone in the field was ready to work the order on the due date and committed to that date. Our internal motto was "TAKE NO EXCUSES; MAKE NO ECCUSES!" At the 20-day timeline, the manager followed up with his supervisor and the manager in the field to make sure that everyone would keep their commitments. That way if a problem was encountered, or even anticipated, we got involved early on so that we could address them and have them corrected prior to the due date. Yes, we still missed a few, but kept 97% of our due dates. You can be assured, the 3% that we missed were not due to lack of effort or desire. Remember we had "DISIPLINED PEOPLE THINKING DISIPLINED THOUGHTS and TAKING DISIPLINED ACTIONS."

Our Goal of "Improving Customer Satisfaction" resulted in a reduction of escalations to the Director and Vice-President from five per month to less than one per quarter. Other groups reporting to the same Director and Vice-President had no improvement and/or remained between five and 10 per month.

We also got results from our "Improve employee morale" Goal. Our turnover rate went from 12% to less than one percent. We only lost 2 of 130 employees—one of them retired. This was an 88% improvement. This impacted our employees and our stockholders, as our training diminished enough to move most of our trainers into production. At the same time, our Dallas Center's turnover only improved by 6%.

Our Goal to "Improve Intervals" was one of our biggest successes. When we started MissionWon™, all of our intervals were slightly better than the other four centers that also handled the CLEC orders for the company. When I say slightly, I am talking about if our numbers were 36.7 days; the other center's numbers were 37.2 days to 40 days. Our end-to-end interval improved by 145%. Our order entry intervals started at 2.15 days. This was the same as the other OE teams (See Figures 5 and 6); which went from 2.15 days down to .67 days, a 221% improvement! During that same period, the next best center's improvement was 19%. Remember I said that this methodology's results are like that flywheel. Look at the quarterly results from one quarter to the next. Improvement from the 1st quarter to the next was 9%. The following quarterly improvements were: 21%, 19%, 33%, 33%, 29%, and finally we reached a brick wall at 0% (See Figure 7). I doubt we could have cut any more time from our order entry process.

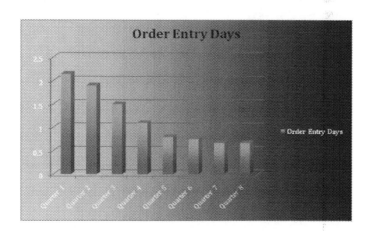

Figure 5

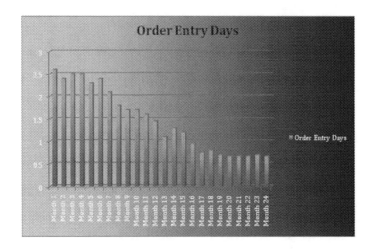

Figure 6

Figure 7

Our order entry manager, her supervisors and their staffs did a tremendous job of identifying and achieving all of their Goals. They were continuously resetting the standards that they set for themselves and the rest of the company.

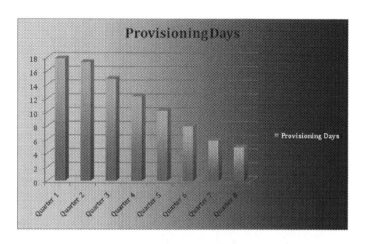

Figure 8

Our engineering/provisioning intervals (See Figures 8 and 9) improved from 17.85 days down to 4.9 days, a 361% improvement! The next best center's improvement over the same time frame was only 16%. Notice on the Provisioning Interval graph how we got positive results at the beginning. But look at the results as we went along. They improved at an even faster pace. Starting with the second quarter our improvements from the previous quarters were, 3%, 17%, 31%, 43%, 55%, 67%, and 73%. Think about it! The improvements were outstanding! Look at the graph that shows the improvements between each quarter (See Figure 10). The quarter represented by quarter five in the graph are when we took over the orders from the Dallas and Fredrick Centers. How many companies do you know have that kind of continuous improvement even without tripling their workload? Remember these results were with tripling our volume of orders! Our local service delivery managers, their supervisors and their staffs also did a fantastic job of identifying and achieving all of their Goals. They, too, continuously reset the standards for the rest of the company. That was one of the things we wanted to do–"Continue to Reset the Standards." Even after we were well ahead of the other four CLEC Centers on all of our measurements, we focused on continually beating **our** previous numbers every month. By continually beating ourselves every month/quarter, we would continue to be the best and continue to reset those standards. Just as Intel's goal is to continually beat itself, we wanted to continually beat our own monthly/quarterly numbers. When I first started, we looked at how we were doing compared to the rest of the company who did the same functions as we did. We found that we were improving every month in every measurement where the other groups doing the same job functions were showing very little improvement, if at all. We then quit looking at their results and only looked at ours to make sure we improved on every measurement that impacted us. Had we kept just looking at the other departments and comparing ourselves to them we would have said to ourselves, "We are good." That would not have given us the incentive to be "GREAT." As Jim Collins says in his book, "Good is the enemy of Great!" My staff was not satisfied with just being good, they wanted to be **"GREAT"**, and they were!

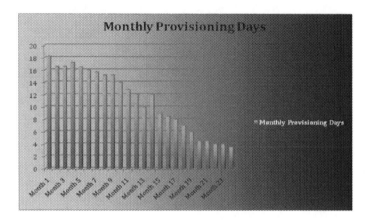

Figure 9

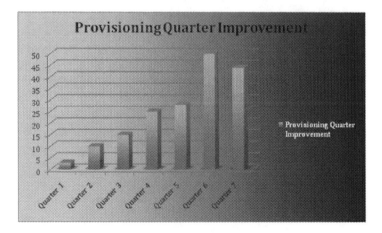

Figure 10

Our end-to-end intervals, from the time we got the order in Order Entry until the customer actually got his service, went from 36.7 days to less than 15 days (See Figures 11 and 12). This was a 145% improvement that resulted in additional billing revenue of over $1,000,000 per month. The closest center's improvement was an additional $130,000 per month. Not a bad impact on our stockholders. Receiving their services earlier and with fewer headaches also impacted our customers.

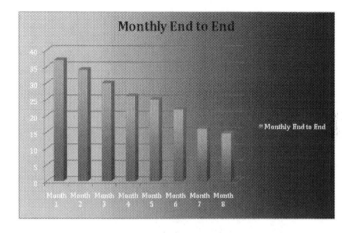

Figure 11

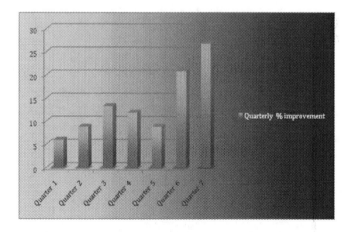

Figure 12

It also gave a big boost to our employees' morale when they kept seeing their numbers improving month after month. The more improvement they saw, the more effort they put into getting them even lower. They focused on nothing else but getting our intervals down and our quality up! If we went a month without improvement, they would then dig their heels even deeper for the next month. Look at the quarter-to-quarter improvement, 6%, 9%, 14%, 12%, 9%, 21%, and 27% (See Figure 12). Notice in the End-to-End Quarterly Improvement graph quarters four and five had less improvement than the other quarters. Those were the quarters that we took over the Dallas and Fredrick CLEC orders. Notice how once we got the flywheel moving, the easier it became to move it; and the faster it was going! Once we got our Projects identified and implemented, we went back to our day-to-day operations. We spent less and less time on Projects; and more of our energy went into our daily efforts of getting our orders into and out of the system as quickly, efficiently, and as error free as possible. Even doubling and tripling volumes only had a temporary impact on the flywheel's speed.

Look at quarter intervals in the End-to-End Monthly graph (Figure 11). If you draw a line at the tops of months one, two, three, and four, then through seven it almost forms a straight line, indicating that flywheel effect. Notice how the percentage of improvement went up as our timeline progressed with the exception of when we took over the orders from the Dallas and Fredrick CLEC Centers.

Notice how the monthly end-to-end intervals show a steady downward trend. We posted these numbers within the Center to give our employees feedback on the results of their efforts. We also had monthly "all hands" meetings that showed that their efforts were really paying off with big dividends. This fueled their morale even more. We no longer focused on being better than the other CLEC Centers, but focused on did we do better as a city team than last month; and did we do better as the Sugarland CLEC Center than last month? The competition between the city teams within the center was competitive, but the bigger goal was how we did as a Center. This made it easier for us to move employees from one team to another when needed. This was required at times; such as, when we had to send ten members of our staff to Dallas to assist them when Dallas had a large turnover of employees and were not doing nearly as well. This included both managers and technical staff for about a year.

What was our ultimate Goal for our average end-to-end interval? 10 Days! Could we have achieved it had we been able to continue? Who knows? No one (other than the Sugarland CLEC team) thought we could hit 25 days when we started. Then when we hit 25 days, no one thought we could hit 20. Then we hit 20; no one thought we could hit 15. We did all of the above and had not bottomed out yet! If you look at the trend line, you can see the 10-day mark was definitely within the realm of possibility.

Based on the above results, two of the other four CLEC center's orders were redirected to the Sugarland center; and they were given other responsibilities resulting in a savings of over $14,000,000 per year. Big impact on our investors! Remember, all of this from about 130 DISCIPLINED employees, when we ended, thinking DISCIPLINED thoughts and taking DISCIPLINED actions!

Let's look at the results from our networking company where we focused our plan around being "customer intimate." This company started by building personnel computers and moved to selling Wide Area Networking equipment and the engineering services that went along with the hardware. They were a $10M company prior to my arrival and had 40 employees. Although I was only there a year, we still accomplished and set in motion many Goals that were needed to move this company along in its Mission. I understand that they are now a $50M company. I don't know whether or not they are still using MissionWon™; but from conversations with my former managers, the person hired to take my place asked them what they were doing. They handed him the MissionWon™ document that we had developed. When he finished reading it, he told them that was exactly what they should be doing and to keep doing it. I can only tell you what we accomplished in the short year that I was there and it was significant.

Lets look again at its Mission Statement.

> **MISSION - "To Deliver Outstanding Customer Service Through Customer Intimate Value Disciplines, to Provide Fulfilling Careers and Professional Satisfaction to Our Employees, and to Achieve Financial Success Through Growth and Productivity"**

One of our Goals was to improve productivity. We set up a number of Tactical Goals and Projects that were in the infancy stages of being implemented. One of our Tactical Goals was to improve our project management performance. To address this, we hired a project manager specifically for our large projects. We also focused more on assigning our engineers to projects that met their interests and abilities. Another project we undertook was to formalize our organization so that everyone, including our customers, understood areas of responsibility. We also set in motion practices that improved our engineer's non-billable time such as, sending our less-experienced engineers out with our more-experienced engineers. This allowed them to gain additional knowledge and experiences instead of wasting time sitting around the office.

We also looked at ways to improve our profitability by raising our prices for our specialized services, such as security and Voice Over Internet Protocol (VoIP). We also trained all of our engineers with specialized training from our manufacturers. We minimized our services that were not as profitable and focused on those that were the most profitable. We looked for ways to provide innovative services to our customers.

Our major Goal for the year was completing our Cisco Silver Certification and achieving our Gold Certification. Prior to my arriving, the company had gone almost through the initial process of completing the Silver Certification, but we had to finish up a few things to finalize that certification. Achieving Gold status was a major hurdle because only 23 companies in the United States had achieved that certification. All of them were extremely large companies such as General Electric. None had less than 500 employees let alone 50! The President of our company wanted it achieved in less than seven months because he had a bet with one of his Cisco friends who said it could not be done. No one else in the world had accomplished it in less than a year or on the first attempt. Needless to say, we had a lot of hurdles to jump. To start with, we had only one CCIE in the company and needed four to achieve Cisco's top engineering certification. Needless to say, they were few and far between because of the high standards and knowledge required to attain this level of certification. I believe at the time there were less than 100 in the United States and there were only three in Louisiana. Luckily one of them worked for us. We hired one additional CCIE and then trained two internal engineers and got them through the testing process. This was our most difficult task, but we had many more challenges before we could complete the extensive requirements for certification. Bottom line, we got our certification on the first try and just made it under the seven-month time line that was the bet. This addressed our stockholders as we now got an additional discount from Cisco. This increased our profits by 10% from our base; but more importantly the larger our volume, the larger our profits. We also got better business because we were the only company in the South that held the Gold Certification.

Another of our Goals was to "Get Better Business." This meant that we wanted to upgrade our customer base to larger customers who could pay higher prices for our more specialized services. Cisco helped us to get a job with one of the largest hospital services companies in the United States. We focused on working with this company and the things that we identified in our MissionWon™ plan to become their only subcontractor of Cisco Services throughout the United States. They estimated that they would do about one million dollars of services business with us in the coming year. Unfortunately for the company, the owners made a decision that ended this relationship by underbidding on a hospital services contract against them, which I strongly recommended against. So for a <u>possibility</u> of getting a $60,000 contract, they gave up a probable one million dollar contract. Go figure! We also addressed this Goal by repackaging our services and focusing more on the value that we added to Cisco's hardware. We also started to market our "specialization, knowledge, and experience" versus our competitors.

We wanted to "raise our client satisfaction" by focusing our engineers on improving our availability, continuing to raise our customer's expectations, nurturing our existing customers, and listening better to what they said. We "added value" and continued to raise our customer expectations by having our engineers focus on:

- Make sure they understood what was "unique" about our customers-- what made them different and stand apart
- Paid attention to what they said and what they would like rather than what we desired for them
- Offered first-class explanations as to what we were doing and why
- Assisted our customers in understanding what was going on and helped them reach their own conclusions, not ours
- Kept them adequately educated
- Documented our work activities well
- Stayed away from unclear terminology
- Were accessible to our customers
- Informed our customers quickly of modifications and asked for their agreement
- Engaged our customers at the most important phases in Projects
- Made customers sense that he/she was key to us
- Showed interest/were supportive to our customers beyond our assigned responsibilities
- Learned to persuade, not assert
- Empowered our customers with rationale, not just conclusions
- Engaged our customers in processes of brainstorming/gave them action items
- Assisted our customers in utilizing what we delivered
- Presented options/let them decide
- Made reports more meaningful

- Sent copies of meetings/project plans/important e-mail the next day
- Made meetings more valuable

Another of our major Goals for the company was to increase our "Services Business." By getting better business and improving customer satisfaction, we increased our services income by 180% that first year. Due to the flywheel effect, I am sure that this portion of the business continues to increase to this day if they continued to use the Projects/Changes that we identified through this planning methodology.

These were some of the initiatives we undertook to increase not only our services business, but also our value to our customers. Although I was only there a year and did not have the time to see all of the results, I understand that they are now a $50M company. Remember, it takes a lot less time and money to keep an existing customer than it does to gain a new one. Nurturing and keeping your existing customers is an extremely important goal for any company, but if you are a services company it is critical.

12

Conclusion

"Leadership. One must not hesitate to innovate and change with the times...the leader who stands still is not progressing and he will not be a leader for long. Leadership is based on a spiritual quality, the power to inspire, the power to inspire others to follow. Leaders are made, and contrary to the opinion of many, they are not born.... They are made by hard effort, which is the price we must all pay for success."

Vince Lombardi

MissionWon™ meets the above statement because it allows the leaders to innovate and change direction as necessary. It assists them in inspiring employees to follow their leadership.

Can this planning methodology be used for any size company? Yes, it doesn't matter whether you have one employee or more than 300,000 employees. The process is the same, but the results will be proportional to the number of employees in the company and the number of them who get involved in the methodology. You have seen the results that were accomplished with only 50 employees in the entire company. Can it be implemented in a single department within a company? It certainly can. You can see the results we attained with the CLEC department. Can you get the same results that we got with the company and the department when we implemented the methodology? I cannot say. The results will be up to you and your staff. The more you put into it, the greater the outcome. I can promise that you will get major results if you put in the effort. The results you get may not be as good as these; but at the same time, they could even be even better! Remember in the CLEC, we dealt with internal customers and only one fifth of the orders in the beginning; but we were able to get maximum results for our employees, our customers, and our stockholders because we set Goals for each of them. The President of the company who had 40,000 employees became aware of what 130-150 employees in

Sugarland, Texas were doing! I doubt that she knew she had anyone working for her in Sugarland prior to that. The Sr. Vice-President was aware that 130-150 employees in Sugarland, Texas had the best intervals in the company by far! The Vice-President recognized his 130-150 Sugarland employees out of his 4,000 accomplished one-half of his yearly goals! What can you accomplish as a Manager, a Sr. Manager, a Director, a Vice-President, a Sr. Vice-President, or a President? I can guarantee you will make serious improvements. And I believe the limit to your accomplishments is up to you and your staffs. The more input of ideas and volunteers for your Projects, the better the accomplishments and the faster you reach them.

Since high-level managers look for benefits from changes and mid-level managers look for advantages, below is a list of some of the benefits and advantages.

Benefits of MissionWon™

- **CREATES A MECHANISM TO ACHIEVE THAT FLYWEEL EFFECT** of continually building momentum and creating recurring results
- **STIMULATES CHANGE AND PROGRESS**--makes employees think about their problems and take proactive actions to solve them
- **FOCUSES THE ENTIRE ORGANIZATION** on accomplishing your Mission--building a team atmosphere between managers and employees
- **IMPROVES COMMUNICATION** through employee participation and by documenting your Goals
- **IMPROVES EMPLOYEE MORALE** when they see and understand why what they are working on is important and the impact they have on the success of the company
- **EMPOWERS EMPLOYEES** by giving them a venue for positive input in solving their problems
- **INSURES POSITIVE IMPACTS** on all areas: customers, employees, and stockholders

Advantages of MissionWon™

- Insures that no time or money is wasted on Projects or Changing Processes that don't contribute to your Mission--**IMPROVES USE OF RESOURCES**
- Since the plan is documented in simple terms and posted for everyone, employees know at all times the direction of the company--**IMPROVES COMMUNICATION**

- Since all employees have input into the process, they have the opportunity to solve their daily problems and continue the company's direction and success--**EMPLOYEES TAKE OWNERSHIP, IMPROVES MORALE**
- Managers track and allocate resources to accomplish higher priority Projects--**IMPROVES USE OF RESOURCES**
- Managers can provide feedback on a monthly, quarterly, and yearly basis to employees; showing them their accomplishments and go reviewing what needs to be accomplished in the next month, quarter, year-- **IMPROVES COMMUNICATION, MORALE**

Remember Mr. Collin's conclusion in his book <u>Good to Great</u>, "Indeed, discipline by itself will not produce great results. We find plenty of organizations in history that had tremendous discipline but marched right into disaster, with precision and in nicely formed lines. No, the point is to first get self-disciplined people who engage in very rigorous thinking, who then take disciplined action within the framework of a consistent system designed around the Hedgehog Concept."

MissionWon™ encourages and gives your employees a way to not only be self-disciplined, but also to engage in vigorous thinking by including everyone in the process of identifying the problems that they encounter. They define the Goals that will not only solve their problems, but will insure that the company will accomplish its Mission. They take ownership of the actions by completing the Project Goals that they identified. This is all accomplished within the framework of a consistent and proven system through MissionWon™. We also suggest that you focus your plan on one of the three value disciplines as described in Chapter 3. Although we do not go into the detail of the Hedgehog Concept as described in Mr. Collins' book, this could be identified in the process of implementation of MissionWon™. We suggest that you read <u>Good to Great</u> so that you understand it and how this concept can be incorporate this concept into your plan.

Most people either are or want to be self-disciplined. Those few who aren't or refuse to step up will find employment elsewhere. This will be good not only for the company; but for their fellow employees, since everyone will be on the same team. The fewer people being pulled behind the wagon, the easier the wagon is to pull. Those who step up and pull the wagon enjoy their jobs because they choose how to pull it and the direction in which they are going. They also see their successes along the way as they pass various places they have never been.

If you are interested in implementing this process, for more information go to

http://www.missionwon.net.

If you look at the results that are achieved by implementing the planning methodology, MissionWon™, the ultimate RESULTS are:

DISCIPLINED PEOPLE, THINKING

DISCIPLINED THOUGHTS, TAKING

DISCIPLINED ACTIONS RESULTS IN:

A DISCIPLINED OGANIZATION CULTURE

APPENDIX A

> **MISSION – "To Deliver World Class Customer Service through Operationally Excellent Delivery Systems, to Provide Fulfilling Careers and Professional Satisfaction to Our Employees, and to Improve Shareholder Value."**

MCI CLEC Mission

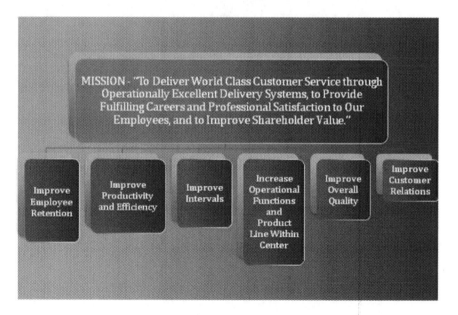

MCI CLEC Mission/Strategic Goals

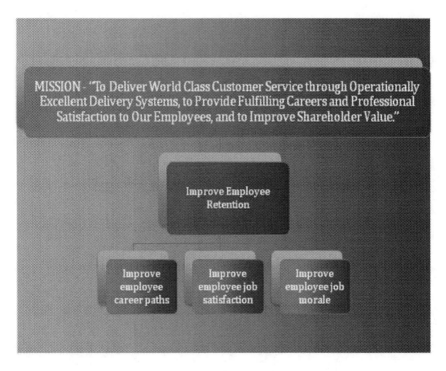

MCI CLEC Mission/Strategic/Tactical Goals

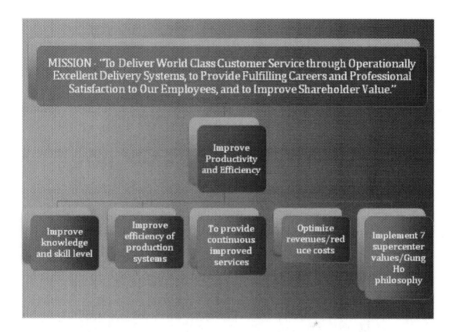

MCI CLEC Mission/Strategic/Tactical Goals

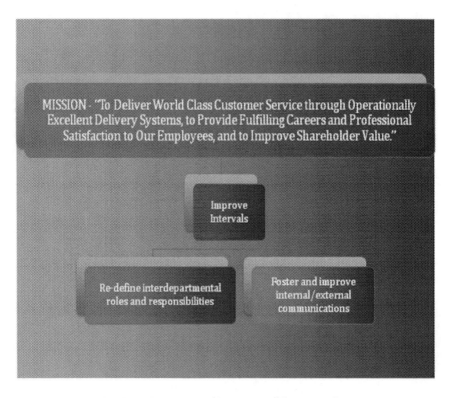

MCI CLEC Mission/Strategic/Tactical Goals

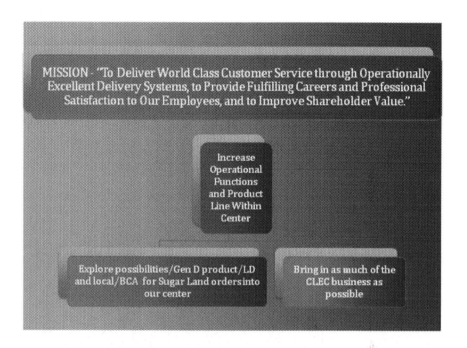

MISSION - "To Deliver World Class Customer Service through Operationally Excellent Delivery Systems, to Provide Fulfilling Careers and Professional Satisfaction to Our Employees, and to Improve Shareholder Value."

Increase Operational Functions and Product Line Within Center

Explore possibilities/Gen D product/LD and local/BCA for Sugar Land orders into our center

Bring in as much of the CLEC business as possible

MCI CLEC Mission/Strategic/Tactical Goals

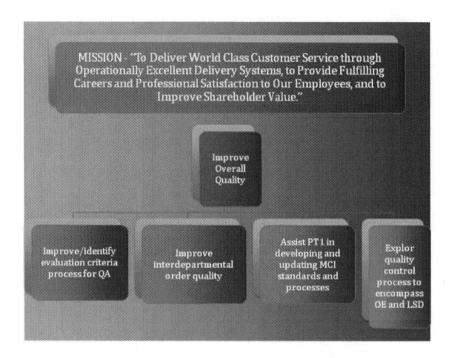

MCI CLEC Mission/Strategic/Tactical Goals

MISSION - "To Deliver World Class Customer Service through Operationally Excellent Delivery Systems, to Provide Fulfilling Careers and Professional Satisfaction to Our Employees, and to Improve Shareholder Value."

Improve Customer Relationships

Improve communication and knowledge base of IE/OSC

Develop programs that foster customer satisfaction

Support our sales channels as our most important internal customers

Empower customers with value added self-service capabilities

Expand communications to market the center

MCI CLEC Mission/Strategic/Tactical Goals

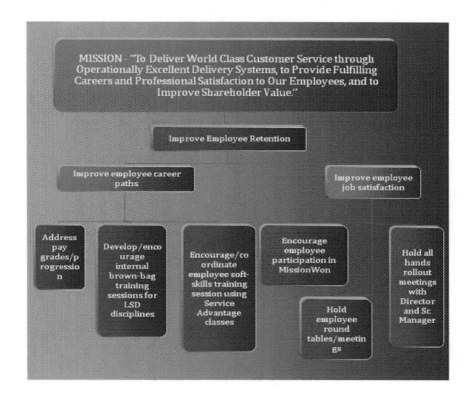

MCI CLEC Mission/Strategic/Tactical Goals/Projects

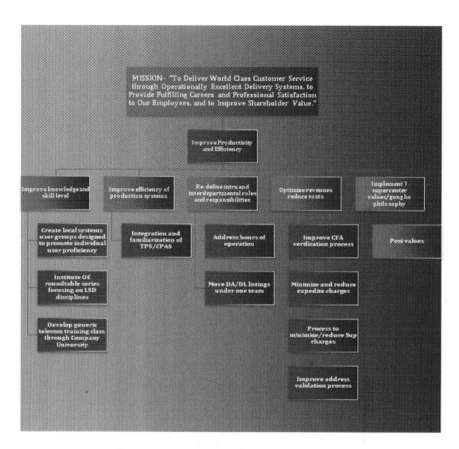

MCI CLEC Mission/Strategic/Tactical Goals/Projects

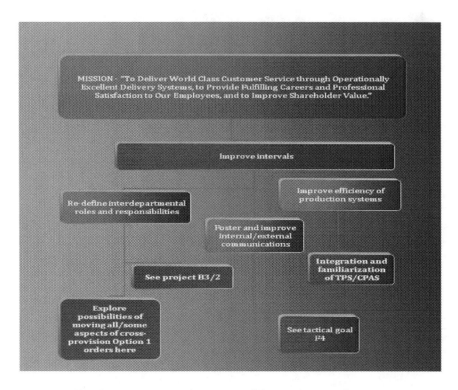

MCI CLEC Mission/Strategic/Tactical Goals/Projects

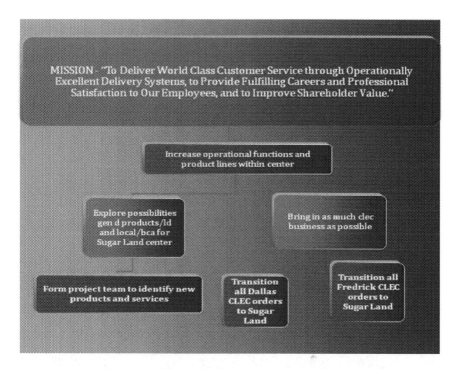

MCI CLEC Mission/Strategic/Tactical Goals/Projects

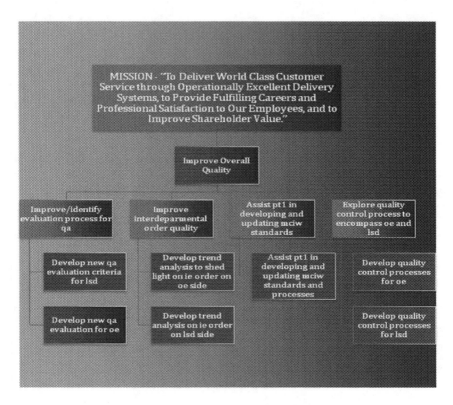

MCI CLEC Mission/Strategic/Tactical Goals/Projects

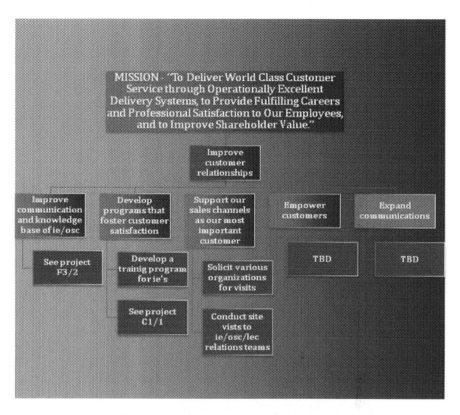

MCI CLEC Mission/Strategic/Tactical Goals/Projects

APENDIX B

MISSION - "To Deliver Outstanding Customer Service Through Customer Intimate Value Disciplines, to Provide Fulfilling Careers and Professional Satisfaction to Our Employees, and to Achieve Financial Success Through Growth and Productivity"

Network Company Mission

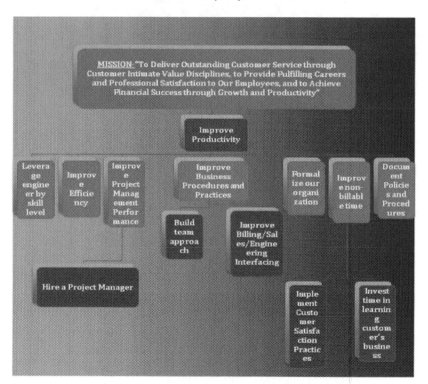

Network Mission/Strategic Goals /Tactical Goals/Projects

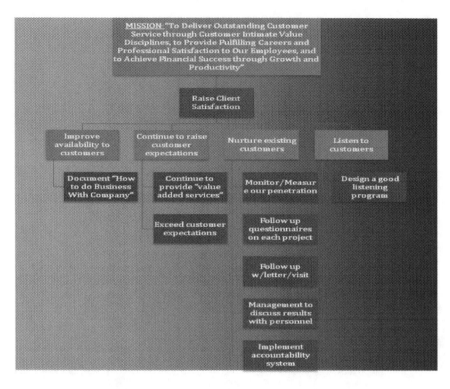

Network Mission/Strategic Goals /Tactical Goals/Projects

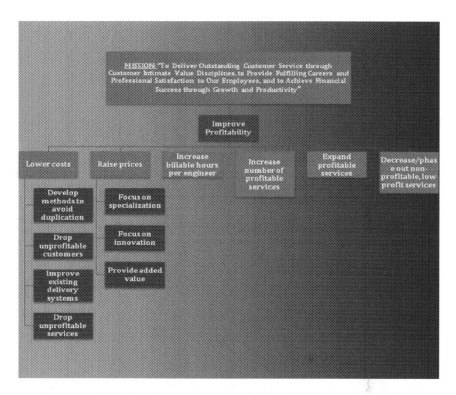

Network Mission/Strategic Goals /Tactical Goals/Projects

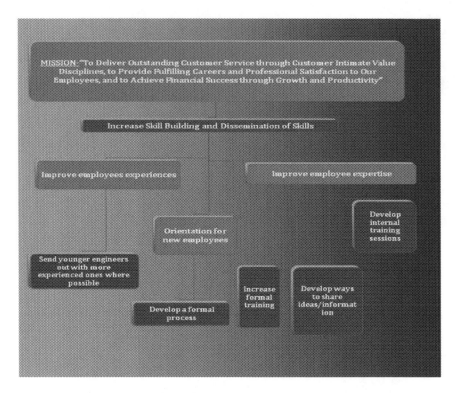

Network Mission/Strategic Goals /Tactical Goals/Projects

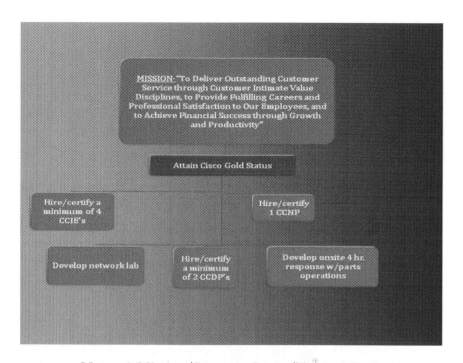

Network Mission/Strategic Goals /Tactical Goals

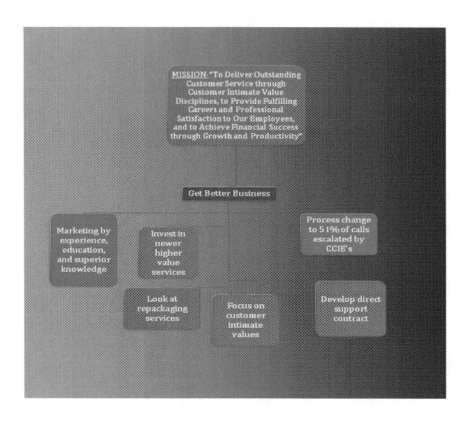

Network Mission/Strategic Goals/Tactical Goals

APENDIX C

MISSION - "To Insure the School Board's Information is Recorded and Maintained on a Timely and Cost Effective Basis Using Appropriate Resources and Accessible to the Appropriate Personnel While Providing Fulfilling Careers and Professional Satisfaction to Our Employees"

School Board Management Information Systems (MIS) Mission

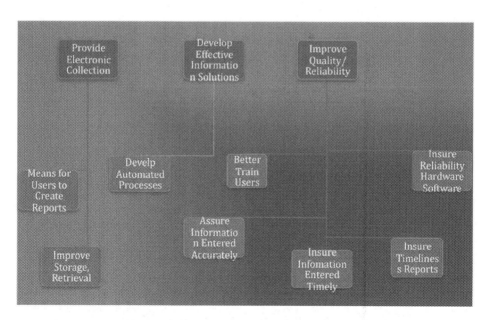

School Board MIS Strategic Goals/Tactical Goals

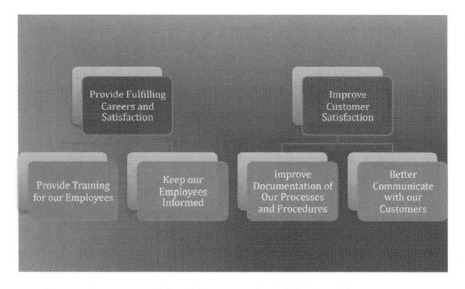

School Board MIS Strategic Goals/Tactical Goals

APENDIX D

Here are some additional examples of *Strategic Goals/Tactical Goals/Projects*:

- Supply customers with dependable services delivered with minimal complexity or inconvenience
- Smooth out demand fluctuations minimize boom/bust periods
- Replication–transfer efficient, standardized services to similar groups
- Return cost of time to clients by making certain our services are effortless, flawless, and instantaneous. (Streamlined)
- Make business easy, pleasant, quick, and accurate
- Make internal and external communication easy, pleasant, quick, and accurate
- Shape our customer's expectations
- Encourage "team" and not "individual"
- Streamline the connections (transaction process) between all members of the order/delivery team which will eliminate duplication, delays, and complications
- IT processes not only track, but perform business processes
- Replace existing student information software
- Automation of information flow processes
- Provide electronic information collection and gathering
- Provide means for users to create their own reports
- Develop/install dashboards
- Provide data access program functionality on Intranet
- Design and develop effective information solutions
- Improve collection, storage, retrieval of information
- Consolidate data stores
- Develop new automated solutions/processes
- Automate directory for customer assistance
- Replace equivalent Swiss w/reports, dashboards
- Update trouble reporting with more detailed input
- Automate accident process
- Automate transportation phone/request process
- Automate customer projection process
- Improve information quality/reliability
- Insure that Information is entered accurately
- Develop cleanup list for student records
- Update district state course file

- Develop cleanup list for employee records
- Utilize filters when designing data entry forms
- Run cleanup customer list
- Run cleanup employee list
- Better train our end users
- Hold user training sessions
- Update company/department Web site with user information
- Insure that the information is entered timely
- Identify due dates and automate reminders
- Insure timeliness of reports
- Develop departmental project schedule for recurring operational projects/reports
- Identify due dates and automate reminders w/escalations
- Insure reliability of hardware and software
- Add generator for backup power
- Offsite backup/disaster recovery
- Provide fulfilling careers and satisfaction
- Provide training for our employees
- Attend quarterly vendor meetings
- Take advantage of in-house training
- External customer training
- Improve employee training
- Improve employee knowledge
- Improve customer knowledge
- Keep our employees informed
- Hold post board meeting meetings
- Improve customer satisfaction
- Improve documentation of our processes and procedures
- Document computer tasks
- Improve financial documentation
- Improve customer documentation
- Document after hours escalation
- Better communicate with our customers
- Document our processes and procedures on Intranet
- E-Mail/Fax customers w/updates
- Attend customer meetings

Bibliographies

Collins, Jim. Good to Great. New York: HarperCollins, 2001

Treacy, Michael, and Fred Wiersema. Discipline of Market Leaders. Canada: Perseus Books, 1997

Maister, David. Managing the Professional Service Firm. Canada: Pearson Education Canada, 1993

See, Kelly E., Elizabeth W, Morrison. See, K. E., et al. The detrimental effects of power on confidence, advice taking and accuracy. *Organizational Behavior and Human Decision Processes* (2011, doi: 10.1016/j.obhdp.2011.07.006

"The difference between a very successful person and everyone else is not necessarily a lack of strength or knowledge, but rather a lack of *DISIPLINE*."

ABOUT THE AUTHOR

Wayne Hernandez grew up in a small town in South Louisiana where he learned many things from his teachers and in particular his coaches who taught him the importance of discipline. By learning discipline from his father and football coach, Herbert J. Hernandez, and his basketball coach, Gene Ponthieux, he was able to continuously improve both his athletic skills and his leadership abilities. He became the first student athlete in the school's history to make All State in both sports. Later he achieved the highest honor in his high school sports as he was selected to his high school Hall of Fame. He was also voted by his classmates to be President of his class from the seventh grade, every year up to and including his senior year. As a senior, he was elected as President of the Student Counsel. The discipline he learned as a young student continued into his college career as he was selected as a walk-on basketball player as a freshman. This team included two future pro basketball players and two players who are in the school's Hall of Fame.

In his career he has been the Director of Telecommunications for the State of Louisiana, Vice-President of a data networking company, Senior Manager of an international telecommunications company, and the MIS Director of a School Board. In each of the last three positions he has used the planning process, MissionWon™ that he developed while working on his Masters Degree in Engineering Management from the University of Louisiana. Prior to leaving each of these jobs, major improvements were made in all areas of his responsibilities.

INDEX

E

effectively, 82
efficiency, 26, 49, 62, 84, 85, 86, 90, 115
efficiently, 31, 109, 122
elements, 33
embracing, 26
employee, 20, 21, 45, 52, 53, 60, 61, 64, 73, 77, 78, 79, 80, 81, 82, 83, 84, 85, 105, 117, 127, 128
end-to-end, 45, 48, 49, 117, 120, 122
energy, 21, 122
engage, 17, 129
engineering, 33, 50, 86, 119, 123, 124
entrepreneurial, 27, 28
entrepreneurial initiatives, 27, 28
entrepreneurship, 17
excellence, 15, 16
excessive controls, 17, 18
expansion, 27
experience, 22, 35, 54, 73, 106, 125

F

Federal Express, 28
flywheel, 18, 21, 51, 108, 110, 114, 117, 122, 126, 128
focus, 17, 25, 26, 27, 28, 29, 33, 35, 40, 50, 54, 55, 71, 107, 109, 125, 129
focused, 16, 20, 35, 50, 71, 114, 119, 121, 122, 123, 124, 125
format, 23
formulate, 31
Fred Wiersema, 25, 155
freedom, 17, 18
fundamentals, 32

G

George Washington, 57
goal, 48, 82, 119
Gold Certification, 54, 124
Good to Great, 21, 47, 129, 155
great, 11, 16, 17, 48, 129
growth, 3, 27, 45, 53, 62
Gung Ho, 63, 88

H

hierarchy, 17, 18

I

identify, 20, 25, 32, 38, 39, 42, 43, 58, 59, 67, 75, 76, 77, 91, 92, 107, 110
impact, 5, 11, 16, 18, 22, 32, 37, 38, 43, 45, 46, 48, 53, 59, 77, 88, 110, 115, 121, 122, 123, 128
implementation, 50, 80, 129
improve, 21, 27, 45, 48, 50, 53, 61, 63, 64, 65, 70, 71, 79, 80, 89, 91, 94, 97, 115, 123, 124, 157
initiative, 22
integration, 26
Intel, 28, 119
interface, 23
invention, 27, 28

J

Jim Collins, 16, 47, 120

L

LD, 65, 91
Lewis Carroll, 31
LSD, 45, 62, 66, 67, 68, 79, 81, 84, 85, 86, 89, 92, 93, 94, 95

M

management, 3, 11, 18, 20, 22, 26, 27, 28, 35, 43, 46, 57, 59, 61, 68, 75, 77, 80, 81, 107, 114, 116, 123
manager, 11, 17, 23, 35, 41, 42, 59, 77, 110, 116, 118
Managing The Professional Service Firm, 27, 50
Mario Thuraisamy, 3
market exploitation, 27, 28
market share, 27, 45
MCI, 5, 11, 66, 68, 91, 94, 131, 132, 133, 134, 135, 136, 137, 138, 139, 140, 141, 142, 143
methodology, 3, 19, 20, 21, 23, 32, 75, 113, 117, 127
Michael Treacy, 25